CANOEING in TENNESSEE

Scenic Trips for all Paddlers

Second Edition

HOLLY SHERWIN

ALPEN
BOOKS
PRESS

Published by AlpenBooks Press, LLC
3616 South Rd, Ste C1
Mukilteo, WA 98275 USA
(425)290-8587

Manufactured in the United States of America

Cover design: Marge Mueller, Gray Mouse Graphics
Text design: Beverly Cruthirds, Cruthirds Design
Map Design: Richard Hirsh
Cover photo: *Canoeing on the Harpeth River in Franklin, Tennessee.* Photo by Cheryl Stewart
Photos: Holly Sherwin and Lanny Sherwin

ISBN 0-9669795-4-0

Acknowledgments

Many thanks to my paddling partners, especially those who offered infinite river wisdom as well as physical prowess to countless miles of river exploration: David Crais, Steve Davis, Freida Demmas, Linda Grassfedder, Nancy Hodges, Jeannie Johnson, Lanny and Murphy Sherwin, Marshall Spencer, Barbara Stedman and Nathan Wood.

Thanks to the members of Tennessee Scenic Rivers Association for their support and enthusiasm, and for providing a lot of great photo opportunities of scenic rivers as well as colorful characters. For capturing those photo opportunities, thanks go to Lanny Sherwin, Freida Demmas, and the folks at Dagger Canoe.

I'm grateful to Roger Waynick for giving me the opportunity to write this book for Cool Springs Press; and to Hank McBride, editor and marketing director, for helping to pull it all together. Richard Hirsch, Graphic Expressions, also contributed many hours and much patience as our map-maker and mind-reader.

My appreciation also goes to the countless people along the way who offered their suggestions and outdoor expertise in helping me choose the best paddling destinations for this project: Mark Anders, Murray Carroll, David Dual, Mike Hansbrough, Tom McDonagh, Mac Prichard, Larry Smith, and Vernon and Cathy Summerlin.

This book is dedicated to Lanny,
who has shared with me his wisdom of words
and his spirit of adventure,
and who believed in this project
long before I had the courage
to propose it.

Contents

Introduction i
A Word About Safety iii
How To Use This Guide vi
Destinations Map and List viii

Section I — West Tennessee 1

1. Reelfoot Lake 2
2. Obion River 6
3. Forked Deer River 8
4. Cold Creek/Chute Lake 11
5. Hatchie River 14
6. Wolf River 17
7. Travis McNatt Lake 20
8. Pin Oak Lake...........................22
9. Big Sandy River......................26

Section II — Middle Tennessee 29

10. Indian Creek..................30
11. Yellow Creek..................32
12. Big Swan Creek 34
13. Buffalo River 37
14. Laurel Hill Lake 40
15. Woodhaven Lake 42
16. Harpeth River................44
17. Red River 47
18. Mill Creek......................50
19. J. Percy Priest Lake........54
20. Stones River 56
21. Elk River 59
22. Duck River 60
23. Tim's Ford Lake 64
24. Collins River 66
25. Center Hill Lake 68
26. Caney Fork River 71
27. Cordell Hull Lake 74
28. Roaring River 77
29. Obey River 80
30. Dale Hollow Lake 82
31. Calfkiller River.......................84
32. Sequatchie River 87

Section III — East Tennessee 91

33. Chickamauga Lake 92
34. Ocoee River 94
35. Hiwassee River 97
36. Campbell Cove Lake ..100
37. Indian Boundary Lake 102
38. Chilhowee Lake 104
39. Little River 106
40. Douglas Lake..........................108
41. Watauga Lake 110
42. South Fork Holston River 114
43. Powell River...........................116
44. Clinch River 118
45. Clear Fork River 122

Introduction

Tennessee is well-known for its whitewater rivers and world class rapids. The raging Ocoee River, site of the 1996 Olympic Whitewater Canoe & Kayak Events; and the Obed National Wild and Scenic River are internationally famous. Rafting companies have set up shop on the Ocoee, French Broad, Watuaga, Nolichucky and Hiwassee Rivers. Because of all the excitement over whitewater, many people overlook the abundance of gentle streams and quiet water lakes that permeate every county in the state. Some are quite unique, like the mysterious Reelfoot Lake that was formed by one of the most violent earthquakes in history. Others are just simple, rolling streams that offer the chance for a day of escape from the fast paced world in which we live.

What attracts us to quiet water canoeing is the tranquil atmosphere that surrounds us as we float down a meandering stream canopied by giant hardwood trees or shaded by towering limestone cliffs. There is nothing more seductive than the solitude encountered on a wide expanse of open lake or the rush of adrenaline as a burst of water flushes our canoe through a garden of rocks. The excitement of these scenic paddleways comes from spotting an eagle gliding effortlessly over rugged cliffs or watching a young river otter playing carelessly close to our canoe. It comes from watching the sun set behind a stand of ancient cypress trees as a great blue heron lets out its raucous cry, or from hearing the slap of a beaver tail on the water as we round the bend in the river. And it even comes from the anticipation of what lies around the next bend, and then the next... that's what this book is about.

When canoeing in quiet water, one can focus on the *being* there instead of the *getting* there. Some of these destinations require no shuttles or portages. Instead of airbags and helmets, you can pack a pair of binoculars and a fishing pole. Although all of the rivers listed are defined as float streams or flatwater paddling, some are more challenging than others. The main criteria for including each destination was that it had to be scenic and suitable for paddlers of all ages and abilities. Although these are both relative terms, I believe that this collection of meandering rivers, intimate creeks, mountain lakes and cypress-studded ponds has something for everyone.

I have by no means found all the very best places. In fact, the more I explored, the more I realized I had only found a few of the hundreds of potential canoe destinations that would qualify for this book. That was both a nerve-racking, as well as a comforting, thought. And I assure you, my travels will continue as long as I am in Tennessee and as long as I can hold a paddle in my hand. Not discounting the possibility of a future edition, if anyone has suggestions of other lakes or streams around the state that belong in this guide, please pass along the information to: Holly Sherwin, c/o Cool Springs Press, 118 4th Avenue South, Franklin, TN 37064. Also, please feel free to inform us of any inaccuracies in this publication, or any suggestions that will serve to improve future editions.

Throughout this project, an interesting question was often raised: "Why would you want more people to know about these unique destinations?" After all, once a place has been discovered, the very reason that it became so popular is often destroyed by the sheer number of people who want a part of the experience. True as this may be, there are far too few people who understand the importance of our still-pristine water resources.

With that in mind, the purpose for writing this book was twofold: to promote the sport of canoeing by making it easier for those who haven't had the time to get acquainted with the many wonderful water resources that Tennessee has to offer. And, most importantly, to get more people involved in the preservation of our waterways, which, like many natural systems, are becoming slowly degraded and often destroyed by thoughtless and unnecessary development.

Although Tennessee has some of the most scenic waterways on the face of this earth, it also has suffered some of the most horrific abuses of its natural resources. Over the past four decades, the often controversial Tennessee Valley Authority has busily constructed power and flood control dams over the entire state, impounding nearly all the major river systems in the name of "water resource management." Fortunately, river conservation efforts are beginning to gain recognition as valuable wetlands and pristine river corridors are being purchased for nature preserves and greenway projects. The public is beginning to realize that not only should these rivers and streams, lakes and ponds be thought of as recreational outlets for humans, but as necessary habitat for wildlife, including many of our state's endangered species. Hopefully, as more people venture out to enjoy our scenic waterways, there will continue to be increased support for future protection of Tennessee's natural treasures.

Tennessee is not only blessed with countless beautiful canoe and kayak destinations, but also with an active grassroots organization dedicated to preserving, protecting and restoring the scenic free-flowing rivers of the state. The Tennessee Scenic Rivers Association (TSRA) is a nonprofit organization made up of members from many states, of all ages, all occupations and all backgrounds. It offers many opportunities for paddlers, such as workshops and seminars on the art of paddling, educational programs and lectures, river clean-ups and conservation updates as well as organized trips to a variety of undiscovered destinations. For more information, or to become a member, contact the TSRA at P.O. Box 159041, Nashville, TN 37215-9041.

A Word About Safety

Although the purpose of this book is to provide a number of easy canoe trips for all ages and abilities, there is no guarantee that these trips are free of danger, given certain circumstances. It is up to all paddlers to understand their own limitations as well as the forces of nature that can turn the fun family outing into a trip from hell. If you use common sense in regards to weather, equipment, and the paddling abilities of all trip participants, everything *should* go well.

However, it is always best to be prepared for the worst, even though you expect the best. Listed below are some of the potential dangers that go hand in hand (or should it be paddle in hand) with the sport of canoeing in Tennessee. These conditions are not to be viewed as discouraging, but rather as challenging — after all, it is the risk inherent in any outdoor excursion that creates a sense of accomplishment and often brings us back craving more.

1. WIND — Strong winds can come up very quickly, turning peaceful lakes into less-than-idyllic, whitecap-filled inland seas. On large bodies of water, including rivers, strong winds can whip up one- to- four-foot waves without warning — waves strong enough to capsize an open canoe. Always check weather forecasts before attempting to paddle out across large lakes.

2. WATER LEVELS — The river sections listed in this book are all rated as Class I or Flatwater according to the American Whitewater Association classification system. By this definition, they have a slow river speed and an easy course with small, regular waves. Minor obstacles are easily avoidable. However, water levels can rise dramatically after a heavy rainfall, changing this rating. Easy Class I floats can become extremely treacherous, even for experts. Some rivers are more prone to quick rises in water levels and flashflooding during periods of heavy rain. Always take this into consideration before canoeing and take no chances. NEVER RUN A RIVER IN FLOODSTAGE.

3. STRAINERS, DEADFALLS AND LOGJAMS — All of these terms mean one thing: there is an object or objects that have fallen into the water and they must be avoided when paddling on moving water. By definition, strainers and deadfalls are branches or trees that have fallen into the stream and have either partially or totally obstructed it. A logjam is a jumble of fallen branches, logs and other debris that may also obstruct passage. Strainers, deadfalls and logjams often occur in the more narrow streams, where they present a dangerous situation, especially in faster moving water. If a canoe lodges broadside against a strainer or logjam, the suction can easily swamp a canoe and may be strong enough to trap a swimmer underneath. Unless the water is flatwater, with no movement, these objects are to be avoided at all costs. This may mean portaging canoes around at a safe distance.

Another obstruction that you may find on any number of streams and rivers in Tennessee is a dam or

Always portage around strainers and deadfalls.

fish weir. Low dams or partial dams are sometimes tempting to run, but are very dangerous since powerful upstream currents (which can hold both boats and bodies) may be created just below the dam. Again, portage around these dams if there is any doubt whether they may be run safely.

4. HYPOTHERMIA — Probably one of the biggest dangers on the water, and the one that most people never consider, is hypothermia. This condition involves the mental and physical collapse accompanying the chilling of the inner core of the human body. If not recognized and attended to immediately, hypothermia can lead to death. Cold temperatures become a serious problem when combined with wetness, exhaustion, and a sinking sun. The best defense against hypothermia is to prevent exposure. Be prepared for an accidental spill or unexpected rain by always wearing or packing proper outdoor gear. Don't let the time of year prevent you from using this common sense. On dam controlled rivers, the water temperatures are icy cold, even in the summer.

5. BOAT TRAFFIC — When the weather gets warm, be prepared to meet up with boats of all sizes on many of the lakes and rivers in Tennessee. Even though non-powered vessels have the right of way over motor-boats, this is one law that you do not want to put to the test. It is always best to avoid crowded lake conditions by paddling only during the off-season or in the early morning hours before boat traffic becomes a hazard to canoes.

6. DAM CONTROLLED RIVERS — Since several of the river trips mentioned in this guide begin just below large reservoir dams, it is important to know how to access water release schedules before planning your trip. The TVA Information Line works through an interactive voice response system which can be accessed through a touch tone phone. All pertinent information is provided in the trip descriptions. Be sure to call ahead *before* planning your trip.

When water is first released from these dams, it will fill the area below the dam rather quickly. Be prepared for a swift rise in water levels if you are on the river or riverbanks when the release begins. Some dams will sound an alarm before discharging water, but don't count on it. Never set up camp below the high water mark along dam controlled rivers.

7. SNAKES — Although snakes do not pose any serious threat to paddlers, except perhaps to those with acute ophidiophobia, it should be mentioned that several of these rivers have abundant snake populations. Summer is the time of year when snakes are most often encountered out of water. Be on the lookout when traveling on narrow streams or under overhanging branches. Water snakes are not aggressive unless threatened and therefore should be left alone. The poisonous cottonmouth, or water moccasin, is rarely encountered.

8. NAVIGATION — Always study your river or lake map before starting out on a trip. Be aware of the trip distance and approximately how long it might take to paddle, given the water level and wind conditions. On some trips it is necessary to carry a map and compass. For instance, on some rivers in Western Tennessee, the channel of the river is not always obvious, making it easy to get disoriented or totally lost. Be aware of forks in the river, dams that may need to be portaged, and any other hazards that may need to be avoided.

9. EQUIPMENT — Having the proper equipment, and knowing how to use it, is essential for boating safety. From adequately warm clothing and rain gear to a first aid kit, extra paddle and life jackets, there are many items that need to be included on your list of paddling paraphernalia. Consider all of the potential danger situations mentioned above when planning your trip and packing your gear. Some things to remember are:
- Canoes and kayaks should have bow and stern lines attached that are 10-15 feet long.
- Bring plenty of drinking water in plastic containers.
- Attach a whistle to your life jacket in case of an emergency.
- Bring a map of the river or lake.
- Have a stuff sack with extra clothing and rain gear.
- Make sure your canoe is suitable for the weight of its load and the water conditions.

State laws require a Coast Guard-approved personal floatation device for each person in the craft, and these should be worn at all times while on the water. Certainly all children should wear them, and with children in the boat, you should wear them too. This way, you can be more help to the children if the boat capsizes. Although many people do not wear life jackets when lake paddling, it is wise to put them on in strong winds or when you are likely to encounter motorboat wake. It may be inconvenient, hot and unfashionable to wear your life jacket, but it also may save your life.

How To Use This Guide

For each lake, pond or river included in this book, there is a short descriptive write-up and map. Most maps show the roads or highways that lead to the body of water, as well as launch areas and other helpful landmarks. Some launch areas are paved boat ramps suitable for trailered motorboats as well as canoes, but many are just pathways that lead to the river. Although the difference is not distinguished on the map, all launch areas are easy-access points unless noted in the text.

The maps and detailed directions in this guide should be used with a good road map. Because road names frequently change — or road signs are frequently missing, especially in rural areas — mileage is indicated to get you to your destination. If you are not familiar with the area, do not rely on these maps and directions to get there. Use them in conjunction with the DeLorme Mapping Company's *Tennessee Atlas & Gazetteer.* The map number listed with each destination refers to the atlas page where you will find the river or lake.

For more detailed information, especially if you are planning on hiking or camping in the area, it is suggested that you refer to a United States Geological Survey (USGS) topographic map. The 7.5-minute USGS maps are also indicated for each trip described. They can be obtained through local blueprint supply companies, bookstores or outfitters. For a list of Tennessee dealers or to order directly, contact the USGS at 1-800-USA-MAPS.

The rivers in this book range from those floatable on a year-round basis to small creeks that can be paddled only in the spring or after a rainfall. Where possible, optimum-use seasons for each stream are noted. This, of course, may vary year to year depending on the amount of rainfall. An especially dry winter or spring season may inhibit the use of several of the smaller streams in this guide.

A few floats are on tailwaters below dams and are therefore dependent on discharge for floatable water levels. Be sure to call ahead for discharge information when paddling these rivers. All rivers affected by release schedules list the TVA Information Line telephone number and the information needed for each destination.

Tennessee Scenic Rivers Association (TSRA) leads trips on Tennessee's most scenic waterways and also offer canoe and kayak schools at all levels of expertise.

Remember that it takes time for discharged water to reach the river downstream of the dam. Wait at least one hour to insure that the water level is up farther downstream.

The size of the body of water described is listed in river miles or lake acreage. In some instances there are several options for the length of trip you can do. Be sure to know your own limitations for paddling and calculate how long a trip might take according to river flow or wind conditions. A river trip of eight miles is usually maximum for a beginning paddler, even in flowing water. Try a shorter length trip if you have not paddled before, and then work your way up to the longer distances.

Please obtain proper use permits and fishing licenses for TWRA lakes where indicated. Also respect private property in regards to camping and launching. Except where noted, all of the launch areas in this book are public. Many are under bridges where there is a public right of way, while others are in parks or at TVA boat ramps. Be sure to get permission from land owners for the use of any land listed as private. By following this simple courtesy, private access areas will continue to be available for our use.

Although this book refers to *canoeing*, other means of paddlesport such as kayaking, sea kayaking and rowing can be applied. In fact, some of the bigger lakes and wider rivers are more suited to kayaks because of potential wind conditions and choppy water that can be hazardous to open boats. No matter what boat you choose, the important thing is to just get out there and enjoy. As a wise water rat once said, "There is nothing — absolutely nothing — half so much worth doing as simply messing about in boats. Simply messing."

Have fun messing around!

Services, facilities and amenities at each location are indicated by the following symbols:

Boat Ramp

Camping

Canoe Rental

Hiking

Parking Area

Picnic Tables

Power Boat Traffic

Restrooms

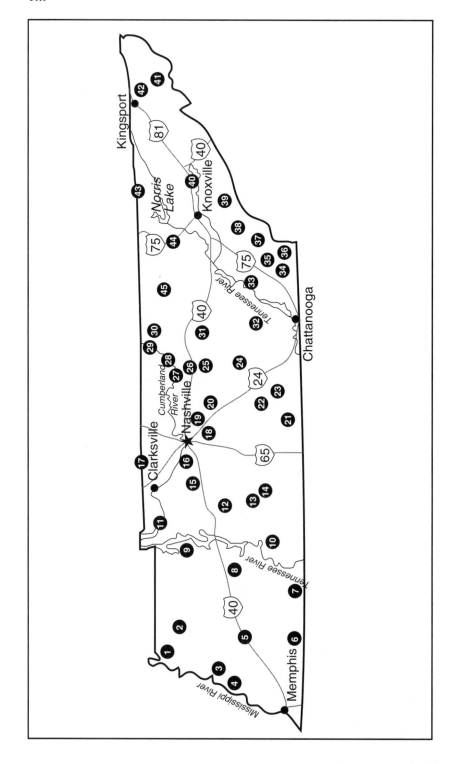

Destinations

Section I
West Tennessee

1 Reelfoot Lake
2 Obion River
3 Forked Deer River
4 Cold Creek and Chute Lake
5 Hatchie River
6 Wolf River
7 Travis McNatt Lake
8 Pin Oak Lake
9 Big Sandy River

Section II
Middle Tennessee

10 Indian Creek
11 Yellow Creek
12 Big Swan Creek
13 Buffalo River
14 Laurel Hill Lake
15 Woodhaven Lake
16 Harpeth River
17 Red River
18 Mill Creek
19 J. Percy Priest Lake
20 Stones River
21 Elk River
22 Duck River
23 Tim's Ford Lake
24 Collins River
25 Center Hill Lake
26 Caney Fork River
27 Cordell Hull Lake
28 Roaring River
29 Obey River
30 Dale Hollow Lake
31 Calfkiller River
32 Sequatchie River

Section III
East Tennessee

33 Chickamauga Lake
34 Ocoee River
35 Hiwassee River
36 Campbell Cove Lake
37 Indian Boundary Lake
38 Chilhowee Lake
39 Little River
40 Douglas Lake
41 Watauga Lake
42 South Fork Holston River
43 Powell River
44 Clinch River
45 Clear Fork River

Section I

West Tennessee

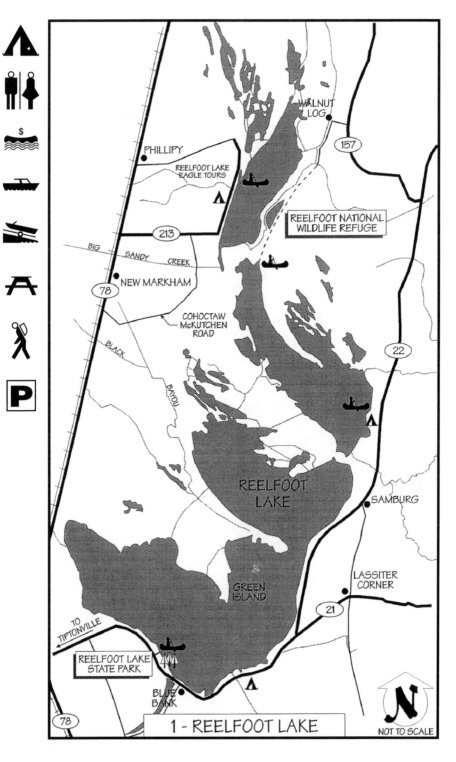

1 - REELFOOT LAKE

① Reelfoot Lake

USGS Quadrangles: Ridgely, Tiptonville, Samburg
Tennessee Atlas: Map 47

Size: More than 33,000 acres
Closest Town: Tiptonville   **County:** Obion, Lake
Best Time of Year: Year-round

Description: Perhaps the most popular lake in Tennessee, Reelfoot is a must-see destination for scenic paddling. The shallow, cypress-studded lake is famous for its sport and commercial crappie fishing. But even during the height of the season, there are plenty of hidden back bays and wooded shoreline to get away from the small power boats that zip around the lake.

Reelfoot has become a haven for birdwatchers, especially in the winter months when over 100 bald eagles take up residence. A nesting population of eagles was re-established in 1988 as a result of an eagle hacking release program. Other spectacular bird species that are observed at Reelfoot include the Mississippi kite, pintail duck, cormorant, anhinga, great egret, large numbers of wood ducks, Canada geese and even shorebird species such as the semipalmated plover and marbled godwit. In addition to avian life, Reelfoot has been referred to as the "Turtle Capital of the World", featuring thousands of sliders, soft-shelled and mud turtles.

The lure and beauty of Reelfoot is fascinating not only because of the vast number of eagles, Canada geese and ducks that grace the lake, or its superb fishing and hunting opportunities, but because of its mysterious origin. The lake was formed in 1811 during the most violent earthquake recorded in North America. Known as the New Madrid Quake, the tumultuous eruption turned peaceful woodlands into rolling waves of earth. Landslides covered many rivers and streams, while a great torrent of receding water tore out hundreds of trees by their roots and carried them into the Mississippi River. Great depressions covering acres of land appeared and were filled with the black Mississippi waters, thus creating Reelfoot Lake. Serious tremors continued to shake the land for over a year, and even today, minor shocks are occasionally recorded. Geologists state that the probability of a major earthquake occurring in the next 50 years is increasing.

The lake was named after a Chickasaw warrior born with a deformed foot that made him "reel" as he walked. Legend has it that when Reelfoot became chief, he kidnapped a Choctaw princess to have as his bride. Infuriated by this gesture, the Indian gods wreaked havoc on Reelfoot and his tribe by creating the quake which entombed them at the bottom of the lake.

Access is available at any number of places around the lake. The Reelfoot Lake State Park lies on the southern end, while Reelfoot Lake National Wildlife Refuge covers a large portion in the middle of the lake. Pontoon boat tours are available for birdwatching, and a variety of overnight accommodations from camping to B & B hotels are plentiful.

Directions: From Union City, travel 14 miles south on Hwy 22 to Hwy 157. Turn right, travel one mile to US Fish & Wildlife Service headquarters/visitor center. The State Park Visitor Center is reached by staying on Hwy 22 into the community of Blue Bank.

Safety Considerations: AVOID WINDY CONDITIONS ON OPEN LAKE.
Ownership: US Fish & Wildlife Service, Tennessee Wildlife Resources Agency, Tennessee Department of Environment & Conservation
Resource Numbers:
    Reelfoot National Wildlife Refuge — 731/538-2481
    Reelfoot Wildlife Management Area — 731/253-7343
    Reelfoot Lake State Park — 731/253-7756

Canoers paddle through patches of cypress trees in the shallow waters of Reelfoot Lake.

The anhinga is a diving bird that will swim great distances underwater, while using its long, pointed bill to spear fish. A rare bird in Tennessee, it can be spotted at Reelfoot Lake in June.

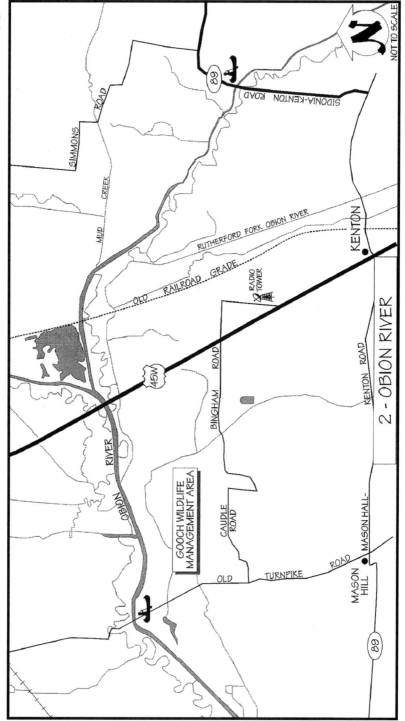

② Obion River

USGS Quadrangles: Rives
Tennessee Atlas: Map 48

Size: 9 river miles from Hwy 89 to Old Turnpike Road
Closest Town: Kenton   **County:** Obion
Best Time of Year: April through October

Description: The Obion River is a classic example of a channelized river system. Long and straight, the river flows like a big ditch with high banks covered with willow and an occasional sycamore. Although less than scenic in terms of vegetation and natural habitat, the Obion does provide good wildlife viewing with muskrat, beaver and even the rare river otter making an appearance. Wood ducks, mallards and black ducks are also commonly seen on the river. Local fishermen angle for channel cat and crappie.

After the spring rains cease and the sediment settles out, the river becomes clear by late April. The clean, sandy bottom makes the Obion River a nice swimming stream. Occasional sand bars provide convenient picnic areas along the way. Since there are few large trees near the river banks, strainers are non-existent. Care should be taken, however, after heavy spring rains, since the river can rise six to eight feet in floodstage, making paddling difficult and dangerous.

Directions: From Union City, travel south on US 45 W to the town of Kenton. In Kenton, turn left onto Hwy 89 east and travel 4.5 miles to access area under bridge. Shuttle cars back through Kenton on Hwy 89 west, turn right on Old Turnpike Road in Mason Hall. Travel 6.5 miles to bridge access in Gooch Wildlife Management Area.

Safety Considerations: USE CAUTION AFTER HEAVY RAIN.
Ownership: Tennessee Wildlife Resource Agency
Resource Numbers:
Gooch Wildlife Management Area
— 731/749-5587

The great blue heron is one of many water birds that feed along portions of the Obion River.

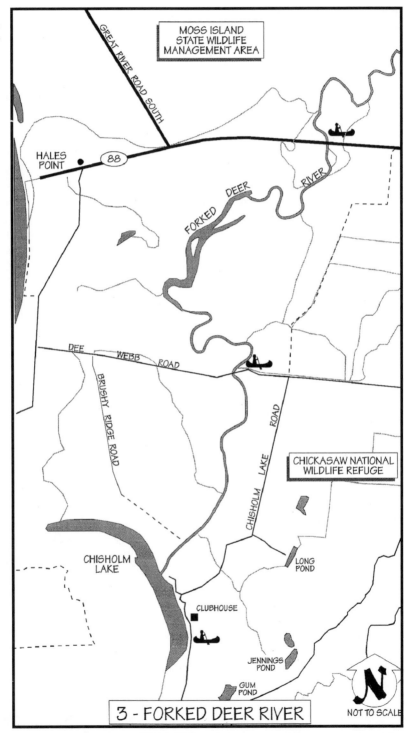

MOSS ISLAND
STATE WILDLIFE
MANAGEMENT AREA

GREAT RIVER ROAD SOUTH

FORKED   DEER   RIVER

HALES
POINT

88

DEE   WEBB   ROAD

BRUSHY   RIDGE   ROAD

CHISHOLM   LAKE   ROAD

CHICKASAW NATIONAL
WILDLIFE REFUGE

CHISHOLM
LAKE

LONG
POND

CLUBHOUSE

JENNINGS
POND

GUM
POND

3 - FORKED DEER RIVER

N

NOT TO SCALE

③ Forked Deer River

USGS Quadrangles: Knob Creek, Ripley North
Tennessee Atlas: Map 30

Size: 10 miles from Hwy 88 to Chisholm Lake
Closest Town: Ripley   **County:** Lauderdale
Best Time of Year: Year-round

Description: The Forked Deer River has been dug into a big channel in all but a few remote sections. These small sections of twisted waterways are majestic and wild, reminding us of what the entire river system once represented. Located between Moss Island State Wildlife Management Area and Chickasaw National Wildlife Refuge, this small section of old riverbed is surrounded by forested woodlands with occasional stretches of cultivated bottomland. Wildlife is surprisingly plentiful on such a small stretch of pristine river.

The Forked Deer starts out rather narrow with an occasional log-jam, which may or may not need to be portaged. But don't give up, because soon the river becomes clear of debris and its natural beauty begins to shine through. The river meanders in every direction, with a few feeder streams to add to the confusion. Navigation is a bit tricky, so be sure to have a map and compass.

Nestled in the fertile bottom lands of the Mississippi, this small sanctuary is subject to the annual rise and fall of the large river. During the winter and spring months, the Forked Deer sometimes flows into the nearby forest, allowing paddlers to short-cut the serpentine channel by paddling through rivers of trees.

The Chickasaw National Wildlife Refuge is noted for its vast number of waterfowl, including blue-winged teal, northern shoveler, pintail, and Canada geese. These birds are likely to be seen on Chisholm Lake in the winter months. Northern harriers can be observed flying over the cultivated fields that border small portions of the Forked Deer. Look for bald eagles in the winter months. Beaver, muskrat, and river otter share the banks with a wide variety of turtles.

The Chisholm Lake access area is located on private property belonging to an outing club. They are, however, open for the public - the launch area and parking facilities can be used for a $ 4.00 fee. The club is open seven days a week.

Directions: Take US 51 south from Dyersburg to Hwy 88. Turn right (west) on Hwy 88 and go 10 miles to a bridge over the second fork of the Forked Deer River. (There are three bridges in a row.) Access is on the right side of the bridge before crossing the river. Shuttle cars to take-out at Chisholm Lake by continuing west on 88 for 3 miles to left turn on unmarked road. Travel 2 miles to left turn on Dee Webb road and then continue for 3 miles to Chisholm Lake Road. (You will cross over the Forked Deer River on this road at another access area.) Turn right and travel 3.5 miles to launch ramp on Chisholm Lake. There is a $ 4.00 launch fee.

Safety Considerations: LOGJAMS AND STRAINERS. CARRY MAP AND COMPASS.
Ownership: U.S. Fish and Wildlife Service.
Resource Numbers:
    Chisholm Lake —731/635-1192
    Chickasaw National Wildlife Refuge — 731/635-7621

Solo paddling on the Forked Deer River

Cold Creek and Chute Lake

USGS Quadrangles: Golddust
Tennessee Atlas: Map 30

Size: 5 miles from Sam Taylor Road to Chute Lake in Fort Pillow State Historic Area
Closest Town: Henning   **County:** Lauderdale
Best Time of Year: Year-round

Description: Cold Creek is a short, straight creek that runs through Anderson-Tully State Wildlife Management Area and into Fort Pillow State Historic Area. Here it meets with the Cold Creek Chute — a five mile long lake that was once an oxbow of the Mississippi River until receding water cut it off from the main channel.

Although the creek is too small for large boats, the Chute has a good number of power boats running in summer months. The Tennessee Wildlife Resource Agency (TWRA) schedules non-waterskiing days on the lake to accommodate fishermen and other recreational activities such as canoeing. No water skiing is allowed on Monday, Tuesday, Wednesday and Friday, and from sunrise to noon on Thursday, Saturday and Sunday. Water skiers can ski all day on July 4th and Labor Day.

Cold Creek is bordered by forested bottomland and occasional cypress trees. The thick vegetation provides a great habitat for many species of songbirds — especially during spring and fall migration. Watch for the Mississippi kite on warm summer afternoons. Coyote, bobcat, raccoon and barred owls are residents in the Wildlife Management Area and are usually seen towards dusk or on overcast days. Turtles are abundant on the lake and on Cold Creek - look for snapping, painted, and mud turtles.

Fort Pillow State Historic Area was occupied by both Union and Confederate forces during the Civil War. The 15 miles of hiking trails guide visitors past the breastworks, restored fortifications and the final battle site. Located on the First Chickasaw Bluff, just past the park office, is an overlook that provides one of the best views in West Tennessee. From this point, one may observe a panoramic view of the mighty Mississippi River.

Directions: From US 51 north of Covington, take Hwy 87 west towards Fort Pillow. Travel 12 miles to right turn on Sam Taylor Road. Drive 5.2 miles to access area under bridge. Shuttle cars to Fort Pillow State Historic Area by going back to Hwy 87, turning right and driving 5 miles to Hwy 207 north. Drive 1.8 miles to left turn on gravel road, just past the office and family camping area. At the end of the road is a small parking area on the lake, but no ramp. Another access area is off of Cold Creek Road. This is a nice take-out if you don't want to paddle on the lake. From Sam Taylor Road, travel 1.5 miles on Hwy 87 west to right turn on Cold Creek Road. Travel 2 miles to the bridge and boat ramp.

Safety Considerations: AVOID WINDY CONDITIONS ON LAKE. HEAVY BOAT TRAFFIC ON LAKE IN SUMMER.

Ownership: Tennessee Wildlife Resources Agency, Tennessee Department of Environment and Conservation.

Resource Numbers:
> Anderson-Tully State Wildlife Management Area — 731/635-7223
> Fort Pillow State Historic Area — 731/738-5581

Mallards are one of the most common ducks seen on Tennessee's rivers and lakes. Like other "dabbling" ducks, mallards feed on small aquatic plants and animals that they strain through their bills.

Canoers paddle along the shores of Cold Creek before entering Chute Lake.

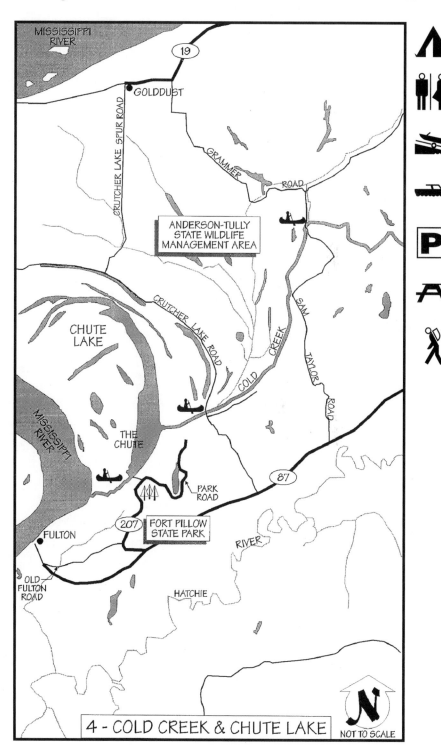

4 - COLD CREEK & CHUTE LAKE

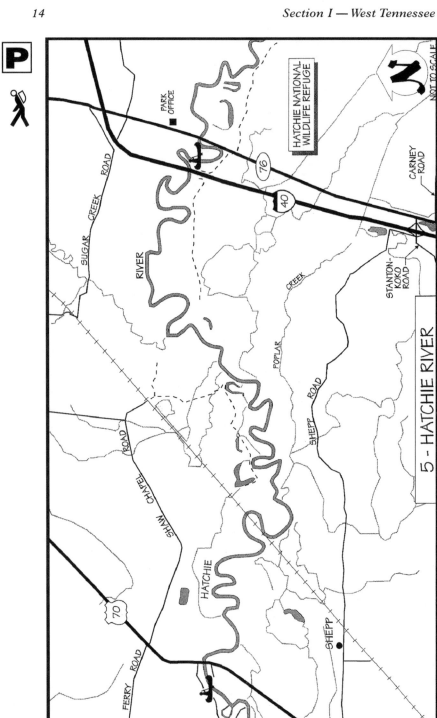

5 - HATCHIE RIVER

⑤ Hatchie River

USGS Quadrangles: Sunnyhill, Brownsville
Tennessee Atlas: Map 31

Size: 8 miles from Hwy 76 to Hwy 70 or 12 miles from Big Eddy to Hwy 76
Closest Town: Brownsville   **County:** Haywood
Best Time of Year: October through May

Description: There is nothing quite like the Hatchie. Rugged and pristine, this State Scenic River is the only major west Tennessee river that has not been dug into a channel by the state in its effort to dewater the land. Unchanged over hundreds of years, the serpentine Hatchie River meanders through lowland swamp, marsh lakes, water prairies and cypress bogs on its slow journey to the Mississippi River. During the winter and spring months when the water levels are higher, the river flows over its banks into the lowland swamp forest, enticing paddlers to weave through tree trunks and low-hanging branches. The Hatchie is primitive and wild as it flows along convoluted passages, with only the songs of warblers and flycatchers and the rustling of small fur bearers penetrating the silence. Large herds of deer often forage near the river, creating quite a sight as they bound through the water in their frantic escape.

Expansive evergreen forests alternate with oak and sweetgum trees along the slope of the Hatchie's natural levee that separates the river from the tupelo-cypress back swamp. Deer, waterfowl, squirrel, fox, bobcat, raccoon, and beaver are abundant and often seen while canoeing the Hatchie. This is also a good place to catch a glimpse of the elusive river otter due to the successful efforts of the Tennessee Wildlife Resource Agency to re-introduce them into their native habitat. The river also supports largemouth bass, crappie, bream and catfish.

Although the Hatchie is canoeable Year-round on this section of river, navigation can be tricky when seasonal flooding makes the channel unrecognizable. Be sure to take along a detailed map and compass. Pay attention to the direction of water flow. Snakes are common and often encountered during the summer season, as well as a large number of annoying insects.

Because the course of the Hatchie is so twisted, travel is slow, and the miles add up quickly between access areas. The section between Big Eddy and Highway 76 is exceptionally beautiful, but quite lengthy, with no intermediate take-out points. It is entirely within the Hatchie Wildlife Refuge. The distance is 14 miles, with no camping allowed within the refuge boundaries. The launch area at Big Eddy is at the end of an unimproved road. Do not attempt to drive this without a 4-wheel drive vehicle during the wet season. The section of the Hatchie River that runs between

Hwy 76 and Hwy 70 is only 8 miles, with good access areas and plenty of parking on solid ground. The put-in is within the Hatchie Wildlife Refuge. After this section of the river leaves the wildlife refuge, several camps and primitive housing may be seen along the way.

Directions: From I-40, near Brownsville, take exit 56. Travel south on Hwy 76 for 1.25 miles to launch area under the bridge on right side of the road. The take-out for this 8 mile section is under Hwy 70. Shuttle the car south on Hwy 76 for 3.3 miles to right turn on Stanton-Koko Road. Cross I-40, then take an immediate right onto Shepp Road. Drive 7.4 miles to Hwy 70. Turn right and travel 1.8 miles to Fin-Feather Bend Road on left which leads under Hwy 70 bridge.

To canoe the 14-mile section of the Hatchie from Big Eddy to Hwy 76, continue on Hwy 76 for 3.5 miles to left turn onto Hwy 179. Go 1 mile to left turn onto Carney Road. After 3.5 miles, turn left on Hillville Road. Travel another 3.5 miles to left turn on Hillville Loop Road. Continue for .7 miles to gravel road on right. Travel this road for 1 mile to Big Eddy launch area. This is a dirt road that will be very soft after a heavy rain.

Safety Considerations: BRUSH JAMS AND DEADFALLS. TAKE ALONG MAP AND COMPASS. BE PREPARED FOR SNAKES AND INSECTS IN SUMMER MONTHS.
Ownership: U.S. Fish and Wildlife Service
Resource Numbers:
    Hatchie National Wildlife Refuge —731/772-0501

Although beavers are common in wetlands throughout Tennessee, one rarely catches a glimpse of the industrious mammal. Look for felled trees along the river bank or beaver huts in larger wetland areas such as the Hatchie or Wolf Rivers. If you catch one by surprise, you might be treated to the sound of a warning tail slap on the water.

6 Wolf River

USGS Quadrangles: Moscow SE, Moscow
Tennessee Atlas: Map 15

Size: 10 miles from La Grange Road to Bateman Bridge
Closest Town: La Grange   **County:** Fayette
Best Time of Year: Year-round

Description: The Wolf River in western Tennessee is one of the most scenic, varied and challenging wetland canoe trails in the country. Within a short distance, this serpentine waterway traverses five noticeably different, yet incredibly wild, wetland communities. From the dense stands of tupelo gum and bald cypress, to open marshes dotted with smartweed, sawgrass and swamp alder, the Wolf River has a wild, almost primordial feel. Wildlife is abundant, yet mostly nocturnal, such as barred owls, coyote, bobcat and fox. Expect to see large numbers of migrating waterfowl during the winter, and wild turkey, kingfishers and wood ducks all year. Easily observed piles of opened mussel shells indicate where river otter, mink and muskrat might have feasted.

In its upper reaches, the hypnotically unique Wolf River narrowly escaped the channelization that destroyed many of western Tennessee's major rivers, as well as a more recent plan to clearcut the land adjacent to the river. In 1995, a 4,000 acre tract of bottomland hardwood and other critical habitat along the Wolf River was purchased after a dramatic, last-minute fund-raising effort that provided the $4 million needed to buy the land as a state-managed natural area. The Wolf River Conservancy was formed to help raise money for the purchase and to oversee the new acquisition. The group is working to put into place a greenway that will preserve the land directly next to the captivating waterway from La Grange westward through Memphis, and eventually on to the Mississippi River.

The section of the Wolf River between La Grange and Moscow is referred to as the "Ghost River" because no discernable river channel is found as the water slowly creeps through a vast cypress/tupelo swamp. Fortunately for paddlers who might otherwise find themselves hopelessly lost, the Wolf River Conservancy has strategically placed reflective markers to show the way. Even though the Ghost River section of the Wolf is marked, paddling it requires a sense of adventure and a knowledgeable crew. Canoes must maneuver over, under, and around many downed trees and stumps. In some sections, the canoe trail zig-zags through tightly-spaced cypress trees and around haystack-sized beaver huts. Despite the extra work in navigating such an obstacle course, it is the most recommended section of the river.

Unless you don't mind getting up-close and personal with snakes, the Ghost River is not the place to be during summer months. Since canoes will be gliding under branches and tree limbs, where snakes often bask in the sun, there is a very good chance for a close encounter of the reptilian kind. Most of the snakes encountered are common, but often large, water snakes. The poisonous water moccasin also inhabits the area, but is rarely seen. Be sure to check overhanging logs and limbs *before* passing under them and use caution when stepping outside of the canoe. Do not kill snakes when you encounter them.

Directions: From Memphis, take Hwy 57 East towards La Grange. Turn right on La Grange Road at the blinking light and drive about one mile to the put-in under the bridge. Shuttle cars to take-out by turning left onto Hwy 57 West towards Moscow. Travel 6.5 miles to left turn on Bateman Road. Continue for 1.8 miles to put-in on left side of the road before crossing bridge.

The next section of the Wolf River from Bateman Bridge to Feemster Bridge at Moscow is a popular six-mile paddle. Although it is less challenging and not as unique as the upper section, the scenery is still beautiful.

Safety Considerations: STRAINERS AND DEADFALLS ARE NUMEROUS ON THIS SECTION. SNAKES AND MOSQUITOS WILL BE ABUNDANT DURING THE SUMMER MONTHS. WATCH FOR TRAIL MARKERS IN THE GHOST RIVER SECTION AND ALWAYS CARRY A MAP AND COMPASS.

Ownership: Private and Wolf River Conservancy

Resource Numbers:

    Wolf River Conservancy — 901/452-6500

    Wolf River Canoe Trips — 901/877-3958

The Ghost River section of the Wolf River has no discernable river channel, making it necessary for paddlers to follow a marked trail through the cypress-studded river.

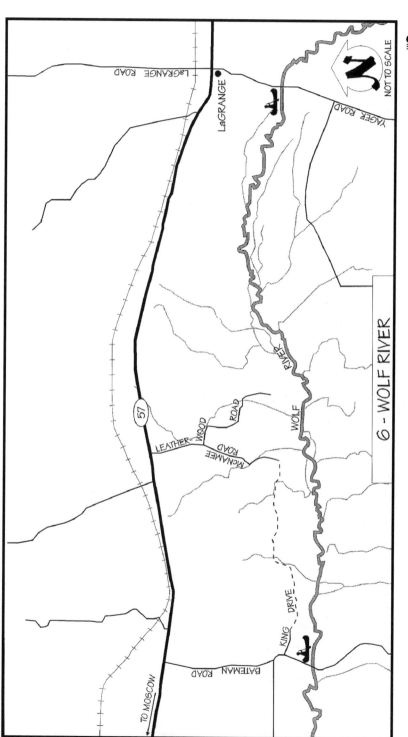

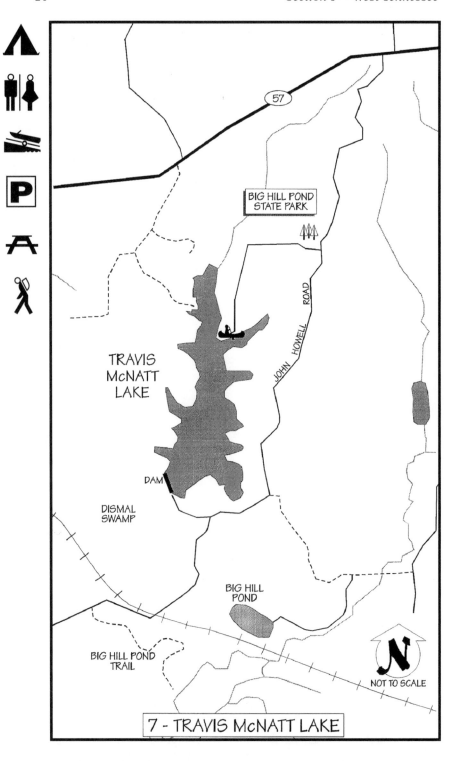

BIG HILL POND
STATE PARK

57

TRAVIS
McNATT
LAKE

JOHN HOWELL ROAD

DAM

DISMAL
SWAMP

BIG HILL
POND

BIG HILL POND
TRAIL

NOT TO SCALE

7 - TRAVIS McNATT LAKE

Travis McNatt Lake

USGS Quadrangles: Chewalla
Tennessee Atlas: Map 17

Size: 165 acres
Closest Town: Pocahontas   **County:** McNairy
Best Time of Year: Year-round

Description: Located in the Big Hill Pond State Park, Travis McNatt Lake is a paddler's paradise. With only rowboats, canoes and boats with electric trolling motors allowed on the lake, the setting remains tranquil year-round. Surrounded by magnificent timberland, Travis McNatt Lake is decorated with colorful foliage in the fall and profuse wildflowers, including dwarf iris and azaleas in the spring. Wildlife includes many species of ducks, the fish-eating osprey, and deer, coyote, fox, mink and beaver.

The park is named for a small 35-acre pond, created in 1853 when construction on the Memphis to Charleston Railroad began in the area. As the land was excavated to build a railroad levee across the Cypress Creek and Tuscumbia River, a shallow depression formed. Over the 130 years that passed since the pond was created, a great stand of cypress has surrounded Big Hill Pond, producing a mini-version of the popular Reelfoot Lake. Although the only access to Big Hill Pond is via a four-wheel drive gravel road or down a 1/2 mile hiking trail, the park does allow exploration of the secluded wetland by canoe.

Nearby is a one mile long boardwalk that passes through Dismal Swamp, offering a great way to view wetland wildlife without getting your feet wet. There are also many miles of hiking trails within the park.

Directions Travis McNatt Lake is located about 18 miles south of Selmer, Tennessee, on Hwy 57. From US 45, turn west on Hwy 57 at Eastview. Travel for 10 miles to left turn into Big Hill Pond State Park.

Safety Considerations: AVOID WINDY CONDITIONS ON LAKE.
Ownership: Tennessee Department of Environment and Conservation
Resource Numbers:
Big Hill Pond State Park — 731/645-7967

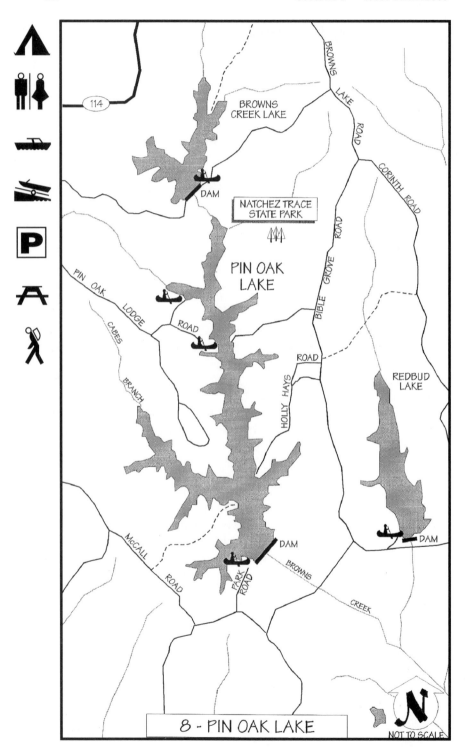

8 - PIN OAK LAKE

 Pin Oak Lake

USGS Quadrangles: Chesterfield
Tennessee Atlas: Map 33

Size: 690 Acres
Closest Town: Lexington   **County:** Henderson
Best Time Of Year: Fall and Spring

Description: Pin Oak Lake and several other canoeable lakes are located in the Natchez Trace State Resort Park. Although motor boats are allowed on Pin Oak Lake, the primary activity is fishing, and all users must purchase a lake use permit at the park office. The Natchez Trace State Park is famous for its tall pines and hardwood forests and for providing a multitude of rustic overnight accommodations in beautiful settings around the lakes. Paddlers can enjoy the beauty of a large open lake while watching great flocks of mallard ducks and Canada geese swim about. Visitors might also see clay crayfish "chimneys" that are located along the shallow shorelines of all four lakes. Pin Oak Lake is also popular for fast-paced recreational activities such as water skiing, so it is best to avoid canoeing this lake during busy summer weekends.

Nearby Brown's Lake and Maple Lake, 167 and 93 acres respectively, are fishing lakes that are managed by the Tennessee Wildlife Resources Agency (TWRA). For that reason, anyone paddling on these lakes must have a valid Tennessee fishing license. Both lakes have rental fishing boats and launch ramps, plus they are posted as a no wake zone. The fishing is worth checking out, especially in Brown's Lake, where several state record catches have been recorded.

Natchez Trace State Park is named after the famous wilderness road that ran between Nashville and Natchez, Mississippi. A western spur of The Trace once ran through the park. Another historical event that has made the park famous is the legend of a pecan that was planted by an early settler girl around the time of the War of 1812. She supposedly received the pecan as a gift from a soldier returning from the Battle of New Orleans, and planted it beside the road to mark their meeting place. That seed has since sprouted into the world's largest pecan tree. The tree has been measured at 104 feet high and over 17 feet in circumference. View it on the way to Maple Lake, in the northern section of the park.

Directions: From I-40 east of Jacksonville, take exit 116. Travel south on Hwy 114 for 2 miles to Park Visitor Center. Lake use permits may be purchased here.

Safety Considerations: AVOID WINDY CONDITIONS ON OPEN

LAKE. USE CAUTION DURING HUNTING SEASONS. POWER
BOAT TRAFFIC CAN BE HEAVY ON PIN OAK LAKE IN SUM-
MER SEASON.

Ownership: Tennessee Department of Environment and Conservation,
Tennessee Division of Forestry, Tennessee Wildlife Resource Agency.

Resource Numbers:
Natchez Trace State Resort Park — 731/968-3742
Pin Oak Lodge — 731/968-8176
Tennessee Wildlife Resources Agency — 731/968-5351

*The largest pecan tree in the country resides in the
Natchez Trace State Park, only a short distance
from Maples Creek Lake.*

*The state-listed six-lined racerunner can be seen
scurrying around the many hiking trails at Natchez
Trace State Park.*

Tennessee's many lakes and reservoirs offer scenic paddling opportunities year-round. However, during the busy summer months, canoers should seek out small lakes where large boats and water skiing are prohibited.

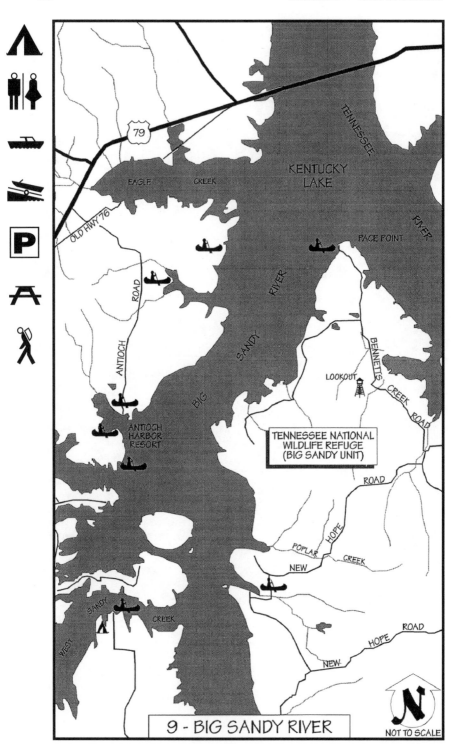

9 - BIG SANDY RIVER

⑨ Big Sandy River

USGS Quadrangles: Paris Landing, Poplar Creek, West Sandy Dike
Tennessee Atlas: Map 50

Size: 24,000 acres
Closest Town: Big Sandy   **County:** Henry, Benton
Best Time of Year: Year-round

Description: The Big Sandy River originates north of Lexington and runs through a channelized stream bed into Kentucky Lake. The most scenic part of the Big Sandy is at this confluence where the river widens out like a big lake. Here it becomes one of the best wildlife viewing areas within the Tennessee National Wildlife Refuge System. The beautiful Big Sandy Unit is a haven for shorebirds and wading birds, with each season offering a new batch of feathered residents.

During the summer from late July to mid-September, when the water levels are lower, exposed mud flats around Pace Point are fun to explore by canoe. At this time, seven sandpiper species and five species of tern can be spotted. Several rare bird species such as the white pelican and American avocet are frequent visitors in the Big Sandy Wildlife Refuge.

Boat ramps are available at Pace Point as well as Swamp Creek and West Sandy Creek. The latter two launch areas are close to Britton Ford Peninsula and Sulphur Well Island, where paddlers can get away from the large boat traffic on Kentucky Lake. This area also offers a wide variety of waterfowl viewing in the winter months, including canvasback, buffle-heads, and lesser scaup.

There are many creeks to explore off of the Big Sandy River and hundreds of miles of shoreline within the wildlife refuge. Be sure to have a map and expect boat traffic during the warmer months. Campgrounds are available along west Sandy Creek and the Big Sandy River. A marina and other accommodations are located at the Antioch Harbor Resort.

Directions: From Paris, take Hwy 69 Alt. to the town of Big Sandy. Turn left onto Main Street, then immediately turn right onto Front Street. Turn left at sign to refuge, then bear right and follow signs 12 miles to entrance on left.

Safety Considerations: BOAT TRAFFIC CAN BE HEAVY IN SUMMER SEASON. AVOID WINDY CONDITIONS WHEN PADDLING ON OPEN LAKE.
Ownership: US Fish and Wildlife Service
Resource Numbers:
Big Sandy Wildlife Management Area — 731/593-3741

Section II

Middle Tennessee

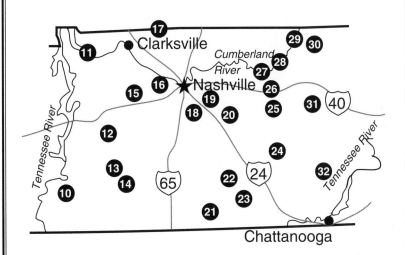

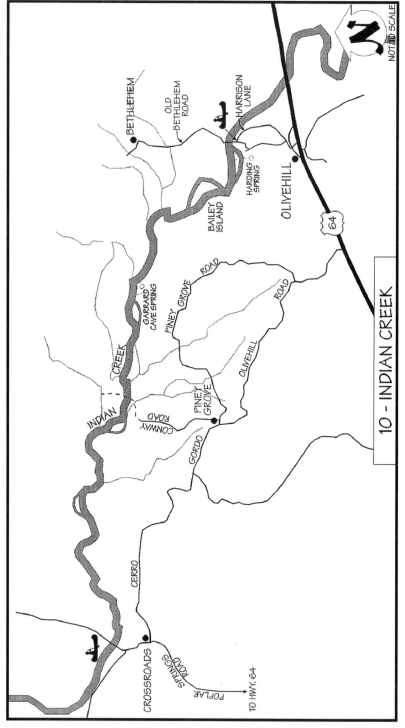

10 - INDIAN CREEK

NOT TO SCALE

BETHLEHEM

OLD BETHLEHEM ROAD

HARRISON LANE

HARDING SPRING

OLIVEHILL

64

BAILEY ISLAND

PINEY GROVE ROAD

OLIVEHILL ROAD

GARRARD CAVE SPRING

INDIAN CREEK

PINEY GROVE

CONWAY ROAD

GORDO ROAD

CERRO

CROSSROADS

POPLAR SPRINGS ROAD

TO HWY. 64

⑩ Indian Creek

USGS Quadrangles: Olive Hill
Tennessee Atlas: Map 18

Size: 8.5 miles from Olive Hill to Poplar Springs Road
Closest Town: Olive Hill   **County:** Hardin
Best Time of Year: November through May

Description: Indian Creek is a little-known creek that runs from south of Waynesboro to the Tennessee River. In its beginning, the creek is lined with enormous gravel bars as it carves its way through a large, flat valley. As Indian Creek approaches Hwy 64 and the quaint community of Olive Hill, it begins to take on a whole different appearance as wooded hillsides and rock bluffs make their way into the scenery. The spring-fed water is clear as it runs over the gravelly bottom. Occasionally, muddy banks appear, and one can see muskrats sliding into the water. Great blue heron, kingfisher, and wood duck are plentiful. Watch for showy Virginia bluebells and large patches of spring beauties.

There are many strainers and brushfalls on the creek, so good maneuvering ability is required. In a few places, canoes may need to be dragged around large strainers that block the way.

An intermediate access is available on this section of the creek off Conway Road in Piney Grove. This is a dirt road with an old wooden rail bridge that crosses Indian Creek. There is a part-time outfitter who rents canoes near the put-in at Olive Hill. No phone number is available.

Directions: From Waynesboro, take US 64 west for 18 miles to the community of Olive Hill. Make a right turn onto Dickson Loop Road (this is less than one mile from the US 64 bridge over Indian Creek.) Curve to the right on Dickson Loop and take an immediate left onto Harrison Lane, then an immediate left onto Old Bethlehem Road. Travel this dirt road for less than one mile to the put-in next to the bridge over Indian Creek. To shuttle car to take-out, go back to US 64 west and turn right. Drive 7.1 miles to right turn on Old 64 Hwy, then .3 miles to right on Poplar Springs Road. Travel 5 miles to bridge over Indian Creek. Cross bridge and turn left onto steep gravel road under bridge.

Safety Considerations: STRAINERS AND DEADFALLS.
Ownership: Private

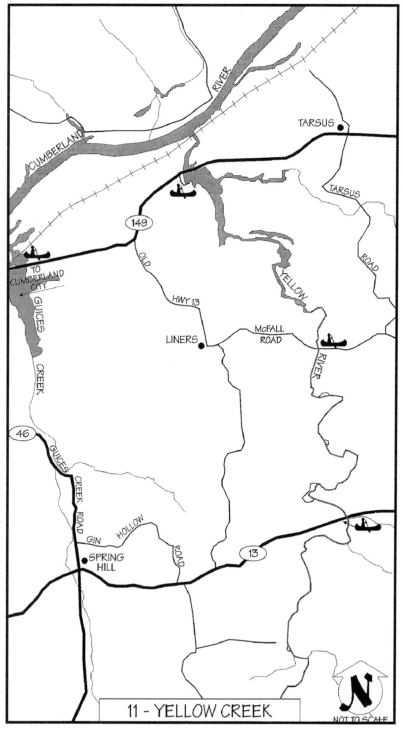

11 - YELLOW CREEK

(11) Yellow Creek

USGS Quadrangles: Ellis Mills, Needmore
Tennessee Atlas Map 51

Size: 11 river miles from Hwy 13 to Guises Creek Recreational Area on Lake Barkley
Closest Town: Liners   **County:** Montgomery, Stewart
Best Time of Year: Year-round

Description: Yellow Creek is a small, canopied creek that winds its way into the Cumberland River (Lake Barkley) below the town of Clarksville, Tennessee. Although the upper sections of Yellow Creek become too shallow to paddle during the summer and fall, the section from Hwy 13 to the Cumberland River is usually runnable throughout the year. Numerous gravel bars and small islands along the river provide nice picnic spots.

Yellow Creek is exceptionally scenic with wooded hillsides, rocky bluffs and picturesque old farm buildings enhancing the view. A gravel and sand bottom reflects the beautiful blue-green water and allows for underwater viewing of the abundant aquatic life. Since Yellow Creek is underused in its upper sections, expect to find an occasional deadfall or brush jam that may need to be portaged.

Wildlife is plentiful on the small creek. Coyote, wild turkey, horned owls, great blue heron, wood ducks, and loads of kingfishers can be observed. Look for kingfisher nesting holes along the area of the creek where there are sheer mud cliffs. The nest holes are about four inches in diameter and are located one foot from the top of the bank.

Directions: From Clarksville, take Hwy 13 south for 2.6 miles to Hwy 149 west. Travel for 10.4 miles to Tarsus Road. Drive 6.5 miles to Hwy 13 south. Turn right on Hwy 13 and travel just over one mile to the bridge over Yellow Creek. To shuttle cars to take-out, continue south on Hwy 13 for 3.5 miles to right turn on Hwy 46 north. Take Hwy 46 to Hwy 149. Turn right and travel less than one mile to Guises Creek Recreation Area.

Two intermediate access areas exist at the Hwy 149 bridge and off of McFall Road. McFall Road Bridge crosses the river approximately 4.5 miles downstream from Hwy 13. It is reached by way of Tarsus Road.

Ownership: U.S. Corps of Engineers (at Guises Creek Recreation Area on Lake Barkley)
Resource Numbers:
Cross Creeks National Wildlife Refuge — 931/232-7477

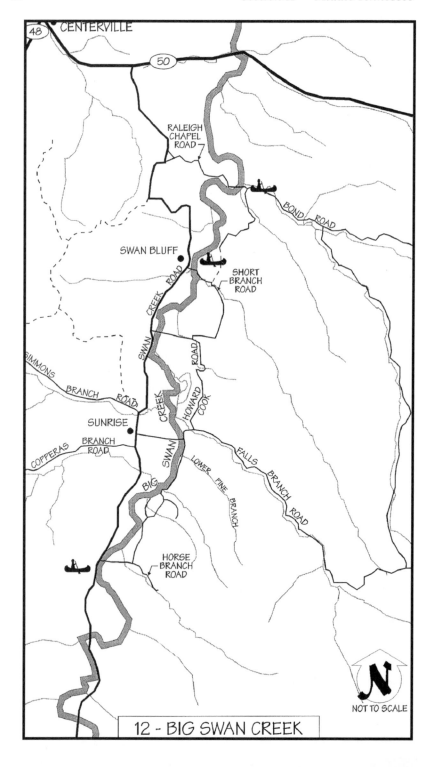

12 - BIG SWAN CREEK

NOT TO SCALE

12 Big Swan Creek

USGS Quadrangles: Sunrise
Tennessee Atlas: Map 35

Size: 7.5 river miles from Horse Branch Road to Raleigh Chapel Road
Closest Town: Centerville   **County:** Hickman
Best Time of Year: November through May

Description: Big Swan Creek is a snappy little stream that provides a nice day trip for winter and spring paddling. Although it is a tributary to the well-known Duck River, Big Swan is one of those "Best Kept Secret" trips that only locals seem to know about. It is a spring-fed creek with beautiful blue-green water and numerous gravel bars. The landscape alternates between high rocky bluffs to rolling countryside dotted with farms and pastureland. The river is accessible from several points along Swan Creek Road, which runs parallel to the Big Swan for many miles.

Because it is an underused stream, expect to find strainers that need to be portaged. Even though Big Swan Creek has no rapids, it can be fast-flowing and requires more technical paddling to get around tight bends and fallen trees. Expect to see a wide selection of bird species including red-tailed hawks, kingfishers and wood ducks.

Directions: From Hohenwald, take U.S. 412 east 6 miles to left turn onto Salem Road. (From the Natchez Trace Parkway, take U.S. 412 west for 2.4 miles to right turn onto Salem Road.) Travel Salem Road for 5.2 miles to Horse Branch Road on the right. (Salem Road becomes Swan Creek Road before this turn.) As soon as you turn on Horse Branch Road you will see the put-in just below a low-water cement bridge. Shuttle cars north on Swan Creek Road for 6.6 miles to right turn onto Raleigh Chapel Road. Go 1.4 miles down Raleigh Chapel to low-water wooden bridge for take-out. For a shorter trip, take-out at Short Branch Road Bridge which is 4.3 miles from the put-in at Horse Branch Road. This is a good access area, except that there is only enough room to park one car.

Safety Considerations: LOTS OF STRAINERS. PORTAGE LOW WATER BRIDGES. FLASHFLOODING.
Ownership: Private

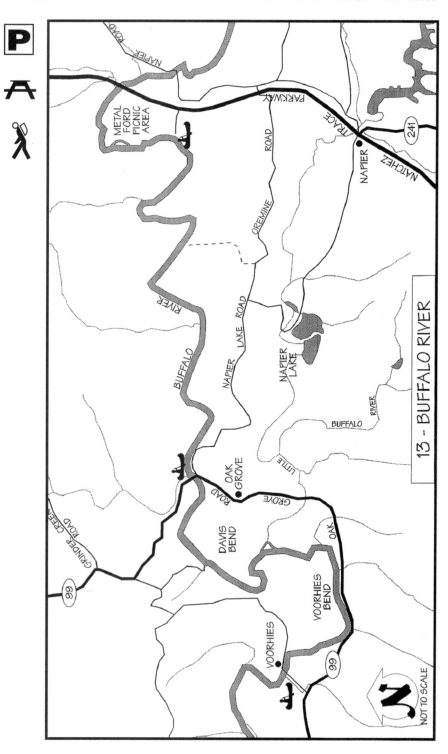

13 Buffalo River

USGS Quadrangles: Henryville, Riverside
Tennessee Atlas: Map 19

Size: 8.5 river miles from Natchez Trace near Metal Ford to Voorhies Bridg.
Closest Town: Oak Grove   **County:** Lewis
Best Time of Year: November through May. Other sections of the Buffalo River can be run year-round. Call ahead to local outfitters when planning a summer trip to check on water levels.

Description: One of the best-known float streams in Tennessee, the Buffalo River is also one of the few that remains undammed for its entire length of 110 miles. With emerald green water and thickly wooded banks, the Buffalo is a great river to run any time of year. Although many placid sections of this river encourage tranquil floating, numerous shoals make the river a challenge for novice paddlers.

Because of its popularity and the number of outfitters along the river, it is best to avoid the "commercial" area of the Buffalo around Flatwoods during the height of their season. The section detailed with a put-in off the Natchez Trace Parkway is less traveled and a favorite trip among locals, however, this part of the river may be low after August and during dry periods of the fall.

Renowned for its abundant aquatic life, the Buffalo supports over 85 species of fish, which can often be viewed through the spring-fed water of the Buffalo. Smallmouth bass, coppercheek darters and spotfin chubs are just a few. Great blue herons, little green herons and belted kingfishers fly up and down the winding corridors, and many species of turtles and snakes are frequently spotted while navigating the Buffalo.

The Metal Ford access area off the Natchez Trace Parkway has an interesting history. In 1820 it was the site of a charcoal burning furnace used to manufacture iron ore. All that remains now is the evidence of a mill race where water was diverted from the Buffalo to the furnace.

Canoe rentals are available at a number of locations down river from Metal Ford. Because of the number of outfitters in the Flatwoods area, that section of the Buffalo River is extremely crowded during the summer and on warm-weather weekends.

Directions: The put-in is reached from the Natchez Trace Parkway at the Metal Ford Picnic Area. This is the first turn-off after you cross the Buffalo River on the Trace south of Hwy 20. To shuttle cars to the take-out at Voorhies Bridge, go north on the Trace to Hwy 20 exit, turn left on Hwy 20 (go under the Trace) and travel for 1.4 miles to right turn on

Napier Road. Drive 4.8 miles and turn right (go under Trace again). Travel 5.5 miles on Napier Lake Road to dead end on Oak Grove Road. Turn right to launch area just over the bridge. This launch area has a lot of room for parking and a gravel road that leads down to the river. The other take-out at Voorhies Bridge is 4 miles downstream. Turn left on Oak Grove Road (off Napier Lake Road) and drive 3.8 miles to a right turn onto dirt road. Drive a short distance to low-water cement bridge over the Buffalo. This access area has enough room to park two cars.

Safety Considerations: STRAINERS AND DEADFALLS.

Ownership: Metal Ford access area is part of the Natchez Trace Parkway National Park. All other areas along the river are private.

Resource Numbers:
Natchez Trace Parkway Tourist Information — 1-800/305-7417
Clearwater Canoe Rental — 1-800/260-5195
Flatwoods Canoe Base — 931/589-5661
Buffalo River Canoe Rental — 931/589-2755
River Rat Canoe Rental — 931/381-2278
Crazy Horse Canoe Rental — 1-800/722-5213

The Buffalo River is designated a State Scenic River because of its clear water and beautiful surroundings. It also offers dozens of easy access areas and convenient gravel bars for picnicking and/or swimming.

(Above) The Natchez Trace Parkway offers convenient access to several rivers in this guide, including the Buffalo, Duck and Big Swan Rivers.

(Right) Besides being a favorite put-in for canoeists, the Metal Ford interpretive site offers a short hike along the Buffalo River where there once stood a charcoal burning furnace used to manufacture pig iron. All that remains of the once-thriving business are the slag pile and this well-worn millrace where water was transported from the river to operate the furnace's air blasting machinery.

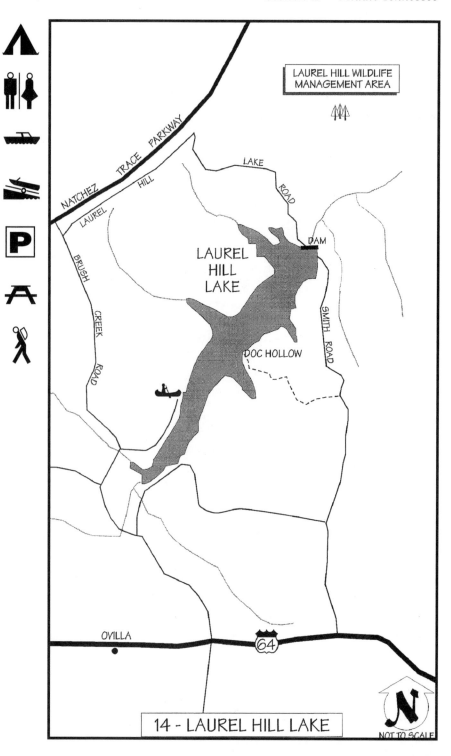

14 - LAUREL HILL LAKE

14 Laurel Hill Lake

USGS Quadrangles: Ovilla
Tennessee Atlas: Map 19

Size: 327 acres
Closest Town: Lawrenceburg   **County:** Lawrence
Best Time of Year: Year-round

Description: Located within the wooded 14,000 acre Laurel Hill Wildlife Management Area, this reservoir is loaded with wildlife viewing opportunities and great fishing. Since it is a wildlife management area, set up for the purpose of managing wildlife for hunting and fishing, anyone canoeing or boating on Laurel Hill Lake must have a valid resident or non-resident fishing license (if over 12 years of age). A daily $3.00 permit is also required. This fee is collected by the honor system during the off-season when the office is closed. During the winter, several species of waterfowl can be observed on the lake including mallards, wood ducks, bufflehead, giant Canada geese and common loons. Beaver and swamp rabbits inhabit the surrounding wetlands.

Miles of hiking trails surround the lake and adjacent forest. The atmosphere is relaxed and quiet, with only small outboard motor boats and non-powered boats allowed on the lake. The nearby Natchez Trace Parkway is one way to access Laurel Hill Lake. A highly recommended side-trip is to drive a portion of this historic route — even if you have to go out of your way.

Though this area is used extensively for hunting as well as fishing, there is a safety zone around the lake throughout the year. Fishing on the lake in your canoe is safe; however, do not hike on trails during hunting season.

Directions: From the junction of US 43 and US 64 in Lawrenceburg, travel west 14.5 miles on US 64. Turn right onto Brush Creek Road and travel 2 miles to Laurel Hill Lake. Additional access from Natchez Trace Parkway, 3 miles north of junction with US 64, turn right on Brush Creek Road, proceed 1.5 miles, turn left to lake.

Safety Considerations: CHECK HUNTING DATES BEFORE HIKING IN WILDLIFE MANAGEMENT AREA. REMEMBER TO HAVE A CURRENT TENNESSEE FISHING LICENSE WHEN CANOEING ON THE LAKE. AVOID WINDY CONDITIONS ON OPEN LAKE.

Ownership: Tennessee Wildlife Resources Agency
Resource Numbers:
Lake Manager — 931/762-7200

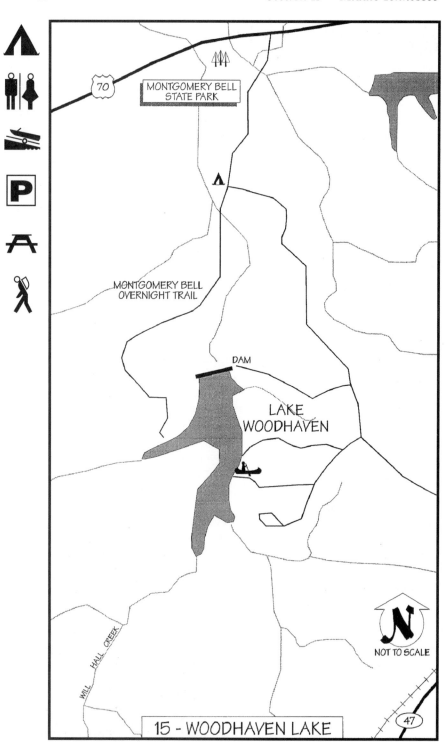

15 - WOODHAVEN LAKE

15 Woodhaven Lake

USGS Quadrangles: Harpeth Valley
Tennessee Atlas: Map 52

Size: 42 acres
Closest Town: White Bluff   **County:** Dickson
Best Time of Year: Year-round

Description: Woodhaven Lake is the largest of three lakes located in the Montgomery Bell State Park. The 42-acre reservoir is small enough to be protected from wind and wave conditions, and only canoes are permitted on the lake. The lake provides a swimming area with docks and a small launching ramp. Fishing is a popular activity on the lake Year-round. (Catch and release fishing for bass and catfish.)

Hiking is very popular in Montgomery Bell, with trails of varying length, and back-country camping available. There is also a 110-site campground in the park, as well as an inn, cabins and restaurant. Montgomery Bell State Park is named for the 17th century industrialist who manufactured iron in the area. The remains of the old Laurel Furnace and ore pits, where men once dug iron ore from the earth, are all that is left of the once-thriving business. The famous 100-yard tunnel that Montgomery Bell had excavated through a limestone ridge can be seen at nearby Narrows of the Harpeth State Park.

Directions: The park is located 7 miles east of Dickson, on U.S 70. From I-40 turn north on U.S. 70 (at the Montgomery Bell State Park Exit) and follow the signs to the park.

Safety Considerations: AVOID WINDY CONDITIONS WHEN PADDLING ON OPEN LAKE.
Ownership: Tennessee Department of Environment and Conservation
Resource Numbers:
Montgomery Bell State Park —
615/797-9052

Montgomery Bell State Park has miles of hiking trails, some with primitive campsites for overnight excursions.

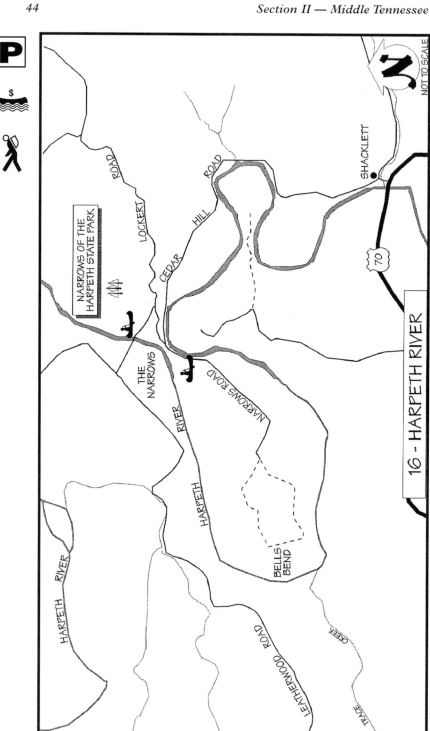

16 Harpeth River

USGS Quadrangles: Harpeth Valley, Lillamay
Tennessee Atlas: Map 52

Size: 5 mile loop on river at Narrows of the Harpeth State Park
Closest Town: Pegram   **County:** Cheatham
Best Time of Year: Year-round

Description: The Harpeth River and its major tributaries offer over 150 miles of Class I canoeing on free-flowing streams. In Davidson County, it is designated a State Scenic River. Numerous fishing holes, abundant wildlife, and an historical flavor make this stream an excellent recreational resource. Interestingly, the name Harpeth is thought to be derived from the names of two local outlaws, Big and Little Harpe, who once terrorized travelers along the nearby Natchez Trace.

    The five mile loop at Narrows of the Harpeth State Park offers a nice, lazy float, with easy Class I riffles. In the summer, when water levels are low, some portaging over shallow bottom may be necessary. Fortunately, there is no need to shuttle cars for this trip. The take-out is just 200 yards from the beginning of the loop and is clearly marked.

    Industrialist Montgomery Bell made the Narrows of the Harpeth an historic landmark after he had a 290-foot tunnel hand-cut through the solid rock. Considered one of the great engineering feats of the time, the tunnel was used to supply water power for Bell's iron forge on the Harpeth River during the early 1800's. The tunnel is easily observed at the launch site for the Narrows and just before the take-out. Bell's grave is located on a hillside that overlooks the Harpeth River and his amazing tunnel.

    A mile upstream from the Narrows, Mound Bottom preserves an ancient Indian ceremonial center. It is believed that Mound Bottom was once a magnificent building complex that had large mounds, stockades, plazas and aboriginal living areas. As with other early aboriginal settlements, Mound Bottom was abandoned for some unknown reason long before the first white settlers arrived. The state-managed archeological site has a mysterious petroglyph as do the high cliffs known as Painted Rock Bluff, just past the Narrows. Group tours, hiking and other activities are available through Montgomery Bell State Park.

    For more information on longer trips, canoe rental and shuttle service, contact the local canoe outfitters. Four-day river trips are available, as well as a number of day trips on different sections of the Harpeth. The Narrows of the Harpeth State Park will be crowded during summer months and on warm-season weekends.

Directions: From Interstate 40 in West Nashville, take US 70 West exit. Travel 14 miles west on US 70. Turn right (north) on Cedar Hill Road (turn is just before the Harpeth River Bridge.) Travel 2.7 miles and turn left to launch site at Narrows of the Harpeth State Park. Shuttle cars back to Cedar Hill road and turn left to the take-out parking area.

To see the petroglyph at Painted Rock Bluff, float the next section of the Harpeth River and take-out at Stringfellow Bridge. This is a 6.4 mile float, requiring cars to be shuttled 7.5 miles.

Safety Considerations: CHECK WATER LEVELS AFTER A HEAVY RAINFALL. RIVER BANKS ARE PRIVATELY OWNED.
Ownership: Tennessee Department of Environment and Conservation
Resource Numbers:
    Montgomery Bell State Park — 615/797-9052
    Tip-a-Canoe Stores, Inc — 615/254-0836
    Foggy Bottom Canoe Rentals — 615/952-4062

(Right) The put-in at Narrows of the Harpeth State Park is a long, steep bank. Fortunately, the park has constructed a handy canoe slide to assist paddlers.

(Below) The famous Harpeth River tunnel runs for 290 feet through solid rock. Here paddlers get a good view of the cascading water which runs out of the tunnel just before the take-out at Narrows of the Harpeth State Park.

⑰ Red River

USGS Quadrangles: Adams, Sango
Tennessee Atlas: Map 64

Size: 7.5 river miles from US 41 to Port Royal Historic Area
Closest Town: Adams   **County:** Robertson
Best Time of Year: Year-round

Description: Rich in history and abundant in wildlife, the Red River is an excellent paddle trip. The river is canopied by tall hardwoods and sycamore trees, with thickly vegetated towering banks and vertical rock walls that loom in the background. Waterfalls, gravel bars and several islands make nice picnic spots, as does the beautiful covered bridge picnic grounds at Port Royal Historic Area. The Red River was named for the color of the river after a rain, when the muddy earth from nearby farms turns the water red.

The little town of Adams, Tennessee, has become famous as the site of the Bell Witch story — one of the most researched paranormal events in the country. It involves a spirit that haunted the Bell family in the early 1800's and even had a documented encounter with President Andrew Jackson. The residents of Adams and nearby communities, say that the Bell Witch is still an active spirit that lives in a nearby cave. This cave is located on the Red River and can be seen while floating the section just above US 41.

The Port Royal Historic Area sheds light on the importance of the Red River to early settlers. Once a flourishing community, Port Royal was the center of trade and commerce. Paddle-wheelers and flatboats carried farm produce down the Red River to the Cumberland, Ohio and Mississippi Rivers. The bustling town had sawmills, gristmills, inns, silversmiths, cotton gins, a broom factory, brick kilns, general stores and the beginning of a business that never materialized - a silk industry. The Port Royal Historic Area offers picnicking, camping, and fishing. The scenic 1/4 mile Bluff Trail begins at the covered bridge and extends along the Red River. Wildflowers are abundant along the trail, as are wildlife sightings. Look for coyote, squirrels, muskrat, deer and great horned owls.

Nearby is an old Indian trail that once led to the Ohio River. In 1837-38 it became known as the Trail of Tears after thousands of Cherokee Indians followed the route during their forced removal to the Oklahoma Territories. The Cherokee Indians stayed overnight at an encampment in Port Royal, then crossed the Red River as they followed the brutal trail that claimed over 4,000 lives.

The Red River Valley Park offers canoe rental, shuttle service, camping and other activities. The outfitters at Red River Valley have access to several additional launching areas both above and below the Adams to Port Royal section of the Red River. They are also willing to shuttle private boats to these areas.

Directions: From I-24, east of Clarksville, exit at Hwy 76 east, towards Adams. Take Hwy 76 east to intersection of US 41 at Adams. Turn left (north) on US 41 and travel for 1.5 miles to put-in at Red River Bridge. Turn off on the left on a dead end road that leads to a small parking area near the bridge. (This is also the turn off for Red River Valley Park. If you use its facilities at this access area, there is a $2.00 launch fee.) To shuttle cars to the take-out at Port Royal Historic Area, travel back to Hwy 76, turn right, go for 3 miles to right turn onto Port Royal Road. The launch site will be on the right side of the road before crossing the bridge over the Red River.

Safety Considerations: DEADFALLS AND STRAINERS. BEWARE OF THE BELL WITCH.
Ownership: Private
Resource Numbers:
    Port Royal Historic Area — 931/358-9696

The covered bridge along the Red River marks the take-out at Port Royal State Historic Area.

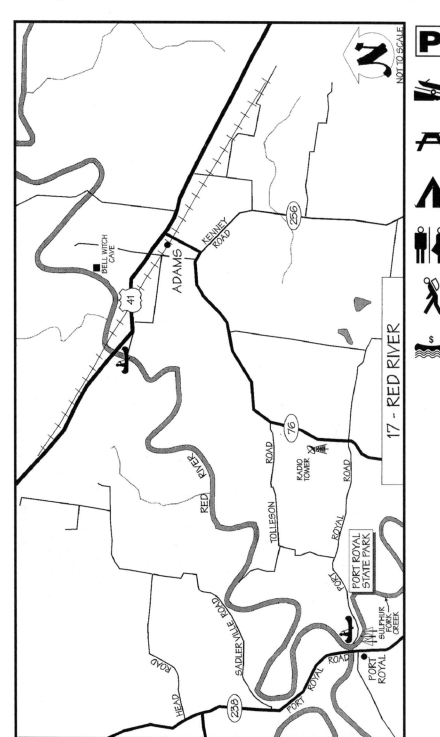

17 - RED RIVER

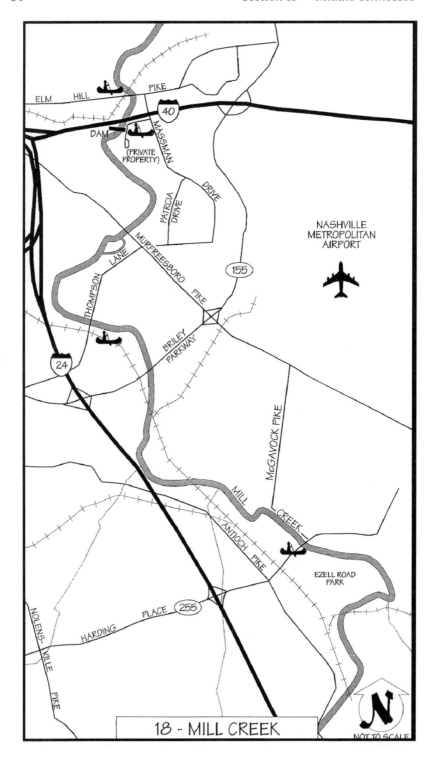

ELM HILL PIKE

40

DAM

MASSMAN

(PRIVATE PROPERTY)

PATRICIA DRIVE

DRIVE

NASHVILLE
METROPOLITAN
AIRPORT

THOMPSON LANE

MURFREESBORO PIKE

155

24

BRILEY PARKWAY

McGAVOCK PIKE

MILL CREEK

ANTIOCH PIKE

EZELL ROAD
PARK

NOLENS- VILLE PIKE

HARDING PLACE

255

N

18 - MILL CREEK

NOT TO SCALE

(18) Mill Creek

USGS Quadrangles: Antioch, Nashville East
Tennessee Atlas: Map 53

Size: 6.2 miles from Ezell Road Park to Elm Hill Pike
Closest Town: Nashville   **County:** Davidson
Best Time of Year: November through May

Description: Mill Creek is not your run-of-the-mill canoe stream. At its beginning, the scenery is pastoral with forested banks and occasional bluffs. Then as the creek flows north towards its rendezvous with the Cumberland River, it becomes a metropolitan stream, passing under large bridges and major interstates as it enters the busy city of Nashville.

Except for the nearby roadways and bridges, the view of the city is hidden behind tree-lined banks that rise up above the river. Surprisingly, it is quite a good wildlife viewing area since many small mammals and birds seem to be concentrated in this riverside sanctuary.

The Tennessee Scenic River Association frequently leads trips on Mill Creek, including its annual Mill Creek Clean-Up to remove the canoe-loads of trash that accumulates along the river banks. During these excursions, paddlers have been known to pull off the stream under Murfreesboro Road and climb up the bank to have lunch at Taco Bell! There is a broken dam on this section of Mill Creek, just before crossing under I-24, less than one mile from the Elm Hill take-out. The dam can be run on the left side with enough water. Watch for broken concrete and steel bars that exist along the side of the dam. ALWAYS PULL OFF THE RIVER AND SCOUT BEFORE RUNNING DAM. The take-out is on the River, left under the railroad bridge.

Not too far from the section of river that runs under Bell Road is a deep pool of water known as the Blue Hole. This is the same Blue Hole for which the national canoe company was named and the area where the first Blue Hole canoe tested the waters.

Directions: From downtown Nashville, take I-24 east to Harding Place (Hwy 255). Turn left (east) onto Harding Place and travel for just under 1 mile to Ezell Road Park on the right. The launch area is in the park where the road runs parallel to Mill Creek. To shuttle cars to the take-out, turn east on Harding, then take an immediate left onto McGavock just over the bridge. Take McGavock to Murfreesboro Road, turn left and travel north 1.7 miles to right turn onto Thompson Lane. Take the first left onto Patricia Drive, then left at the 4-way stop onto Massman Road. Cross I-40, then turn left onto Elm Hill Pike at the light. Take-out is on the right after crossing the bridge. This is a steep embankment which requires some effort to recover canoes.

A shorter trip of 3.8 river miles begins at the put-in off Thompson Lane on the southwest side of the bridge. A large field provides adequate parking.

Safety Considerations: STRAINERS. PORTAGE AT BROKEN DAM. TOO MUCH FAST FOOD CAN BE BAD FOR YOUR HEALTH.

Ownership: Private

Resource Numbers:

U.S. Corps of Engineers : gauging station information — 615/736-7161 (minimum runnable water level is 125 cubic feet per second at the Antioch gauge.)

A large group of Tennessee Scenic River Association members getting organized to float Mill Creek on a blustery February weekend.

Many rivers in Tennessee have the remains of old mills and dams that once flourished near large cities and along major trade routes. Most are just crumbled remains, while a few still operate as mills or Bed & Breakfast Inns. The Walterhill Mill on the Stones River is just an empty shell, but the large dam remains intact.

The Mill Creek clean-up, organized by TSRA, is an annual event, attended by paddlers, scout troops and the occasional politician. It's a lot of fun — one never knows what treasures might be found!

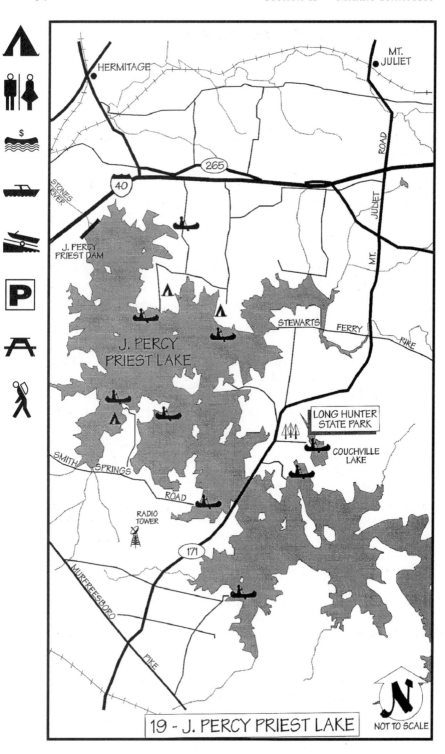

19 - J. PERCY PRIEST LAKE

NOT TO SCALE

J. Percy Priest Lake

USGS Quadrangles: Hermitage, LaVergne, Gladeville
Tennessee Atlas: Map 53, 54

Size: 42 miles long, 14,200 acres
Closest Town: Donelson   **County:** Davidson, Rutherford
Best Time of Year: Year-round

Description: The J. Percy Priest Lake is a U.S. Corps of Engineers impoundment of the historic Stones River and is located just east of Nashville. The lake is very popular among boaters, and rightfully so. It has many wonderful amenities — both natural and man-made. Percy Priest has some highland reservoir aspects with high bluffs in places, and many islands scattered throughout. It is river-like in its upper section where the Stones River flows in, yet wide and deep near the dam, offering large expanses of open water.

The lake is well-endowed with twenty recreation facilities, three marinas, six campgrounds, twenty-two launching sites, one county park and one state park. Long Hunter State Park, located on the eastern shore, is a wonderful access area to Percy Priest. Besides boating facilities, Long Hunter has nearly 20 miles of hiking trails that reach a full complement of native middle Tennessee habitats, including dry hardwood forests, red cedar forests, cedar glades and prairie land. A rare population of pure white (gray) squirrels inhabits Long Hunter State Park. The state park also has its own body of water — the 100 acre Couchville Lake. This lake is open to boating, however there is no launch ramp, so canoes need to be carried 50 yards from the parking area to the lake. When winds are too strong to paddle on the larger Percy Priest, the protected Couchville Lake offers a nice back-up plan for canoeing. Long Hunter State Park rents canoes from mid-April through August for paddling on Couchville Lake. Fishing is good on both Percy Priest Reservoir and Couchville Lake.

Directions: Percy Priest is 10 miles east of downtown Nashville, adjacent to and south of I-40. The other major access road is US 41 (Murfreesboro Road) which runs along the western border of Percy Priest.

Safety Considerations: BOAT TRAFFIC. AVOID WINDY CONDITIONS ON OPEN LAKE.
Ownership: U.S. Corps of Engineers
Resource Numbers:
   Resource Manager Percy Priest — 615/889-1975
   Long Hunter State Park — 615/885-2422

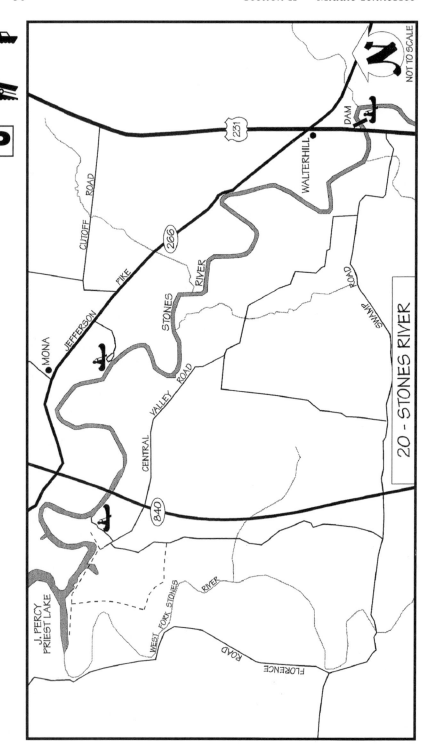

20 - STONES RIVER

⑳ Stones River — East Fork

USGS Quadrangles: Walterhill
Tennessee Atlas: Map 38

Size: 6.4 river miles from Walterhill Dam to Mona Recreation Area
Closest Town: Walterhill   **County:** Rutherford
Best Time of Year: Year-round

Description: The east fork of the Stones River is a spectacular Class I stream which can be run for 42 miles from its headwaters just east of Woodbury to the Percy Priest Reservoir. The heavily wooded banks and irregular limestone bluffs provide the perfect setting for a canoe trip. Because of the many dams and strainers along the upper east fork of the Stones River, a good place to begin is the free-flowing section of river from Walterhill Dam to Percy Priest Lake. The deeper water just before Walterhill Dam is a popular swimming hole for locals throughout the summer. It is also a known fishing spot — great for catching smallmouth bass, bream and catfish. The Stones River is noted for outstanding striped bass fishing. (A State Record catch on the Stones weighed in at 2 lbs, 8 oz.) The wildlife along the Stones River is abundant, with beaver, mink, squirrels, herons and wood ducks making frequent appearances.

The Stones River System is said to be the most historical float trip in the State of Tennessee. All three forks of the Stones River have many small dams and remnants of the mills that once sold waterground flour and other items. The Readyville Mill, on the east fork of the Stones River, is still standing and is being considered for purchase and renovation by the local historical society. The middle fork flows past the Stones River National Battlefield, where 13,000 Union soldiers and 10,000 Confederates were killed or wounded between December 31, 1862 and January 2, 1863.

Directions: From Interstate 24 south of Nashville, take Hwy 96 east (Franklin Road exit) towards Murfreesboro. Travel 2.5 miles to Hwy 231 north. Stay straight on Hwy 231 north and travel 7.5 miles to bridge over the Stones River at the Walterhill Dam. Launch canoes at park-side area before crossing the bridge. Shuttle cars 6.4 miles to take-out at Mona Ramp off Jefferson Pike or 6.2 miles to the East Fork Recreation Area.

Safety Considerations: STRAINERS. FLASH FLOODING. BOAT TRAFFIC BELOW MONA RAMP.
Ownership: Private until Mona Ramp. Below Mona Ramp — U.S. Corps of Engineers.
Resource Numbers:
Resource Manager at Percy Priest Lake — 615/889-1975

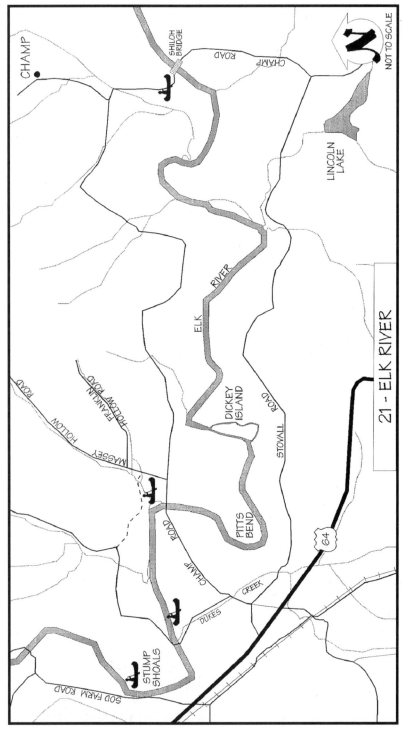

21 - ELK RIVER

21 Elk River

USGS Quadrangles: Mulberry
Tennessee Atlas: Map 22

Size: 8.2 river miles from Shiloh Bridge access to Champ Road
Closest Town: Kelso   **County:** Lincoln
Best Time of Year: Year-round

Description: The Elk River is a friendly, pastoral float stream with good access points and a varied landscape. On the section below Tims' Ford Dam, the Elk is bordered by high, rocky cliffs in some places and wooded hillsides in others. But for the most part, it is bordered by tilled bottomlands with the occasional cow herd encroaching on the riverside. Large gravel bars and a few islands along the way make great lunch spots. One large island known as Dickey Island is a worthwhile camping area. Be sure to camp above the high water line, as water levels rise when generators are running at Tim's Ford Dam

Though the Elk River is dam controlled, there is always enough water in the river to paddle. Remember that when generators are releasing, the river can be a bit pushy — call ahead to the TVA Information Line for water release schedules. Phone 1-800/238-2264. Press (4) for water release schedules. Press (50) for Tim's Ford Dam. Press (#) for future release schedule.

There is an outfitter in Kelso that will rent canoes and provide shuttle service for canoers during the spring, summer and fall seasons.

Directions: From Fayetteville, take Hwy 64 east towards Winchester. Travel 4.5 miles past the intersection of Hwy 50, then turn left onto Champ Rd. (After 1 mile, you will cross the Elk River at the take-out.) Continue on Champ Road for 5.5 miles from the take-out to second crossing of the river at "Shiloh Bridge Elk River Access." Parking area is before crossing the bridge on the left. For a longer canoe trip, two additional take-outs are illustrated on the map. The Duke's Creek take-out is 1.3 miles downriver and the Sod Farm Road take-out is an additional 1 mile.

Safety Considerations:
OCCASIONAL STRAINERS
Ownership: Private
Resource Numbers:
Elk River Canoe Rental —
931/937-6886

Nearby Fall's Mill still sells stone-ground flour and conducts tours of the facility.

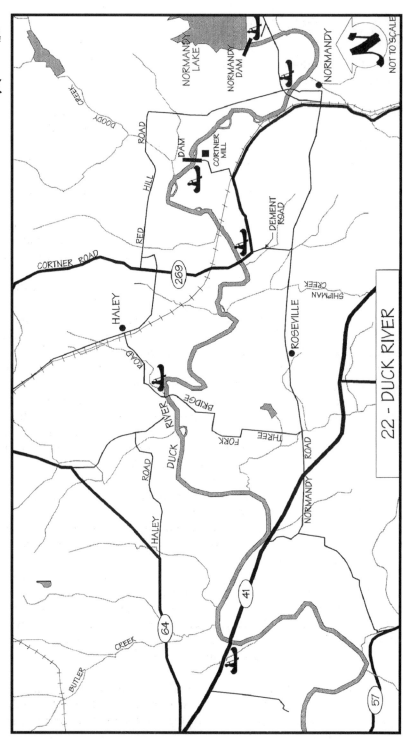

22 Duck River

USGS Quadrangles: Normandy
Tennessee Atlas: Map 22

Size: 12.1 river miles from Normandy Dam to U.S. 41 bridge. Or 7.6 river miles from Parish Patch Inn at Cortner Mill to US 41 Bridge
Closest Town: Normandy   **County:** Bedford
Best Time of Year: Year-round

Description: The Duck River is a lovely Tennessee float stream, offering many miles of meandering Class I water for canoeing. One of the nicest sections of the river is below the TVA Normandy Lake Dam near the quiet little town of Normandy. This section of the river has a great abundance of ducks — wood ducks, black ducks and mallard ducks, and good trout fishing. There are also plenty of beaver and mink to be seen and a vast array of other bird life, including pileated woodpeckers, kingfishers and great blue herons. There is no need to worry about lack of water during the summer months since the Normandy Dam is always generating. However, the river can get too high to run after a heavy rain since there are many small tributaries that run into the Duck River.

If you start the trip below Normandy Dam, be on the lookout for the Cortner Mill Dam, which is about four miles down river from Normandy Lake. You should keep to river right and take out just before the dam. There is a rocky path that leads around the dam. It is steep, but very short. If you don't mind scraping your canoe bottom, you can just drag it down the incline into the water below the dam. Many people put in at this sight, to avoid the portage and to cut the trip down to under eight miles.

Cortner Mill is part of the 300 acre Parish Patch Farm and Inn. Owners, David and Claudia Hazelwood are kind enough to let canoers access the river from their property. The Parish Patch Inn serves dinner and Sunday brunch in a large dining room that overlooks the river. They will also serve lunch for groups or pack box lunches. This needs to be arranged ahead of time.

The entire river has big, beautiful rock bluffs and forested hillsides. Here and there are a few muddy farm banks with cows grazing on the river, but other than that, it is secluded and pristine. The section of the Duck below the dam is also an excellent fishing stream. It is stocked with rainbow and brown trout. Large saugeye and muskie can be fished out of the Duck, in addition to bass, bream, crappie and stripe.

Directions: From Shelbyville, take US Alt. 41 south. From the intersection of Hwy 64, go 3 miles and turn right on Normandy Road. Travel 5 miles to the small town of Normandy. Just over the railroad tracks, turn left and drive 2 miles to put-in just below Normandy Dam. The ramp and parking area are on the left side of the road. Drive 9 miles back to the bridge over US 41 for shuttle. To cut about five miles off the river trip, put in below Cortner Mill Dam.

Safety Considerations: PORTAGE REQUIRED AT CORTNER MILL DAM. FLASH FLOODING.
Ownership: Private
Resource Numbers:
>TVA Information Line for release schedules — 1-800/238-2264.
>>Press (4) for water release category and (56) for Normandy Dam. Press (#) for future release schedule.
>Parish Patch Inn at Cortner Mill — 931/857-3018
>River Rat Canoe Rental — 931/381-2278
>Forest Landing Canoe Livery — 931/364-7874

Be creative! Driving a shuttle can be tricky when there is only one car. In this case, a mountain bike solves the problem.

Cortner's Mill offers fine dining and a few rustic rooms for rent. Paddlers often begin their Duck River trip below the dam to avoid having to portage canoes down a steep bank.

Wood ducks are commonly seen in wooded swamps, rvers and ponds across Tennessee. The male has a bizarre face pattern and rainbow iridescence that is quite unique, while the female is a dull brown. Wood ducks often perch in trees.

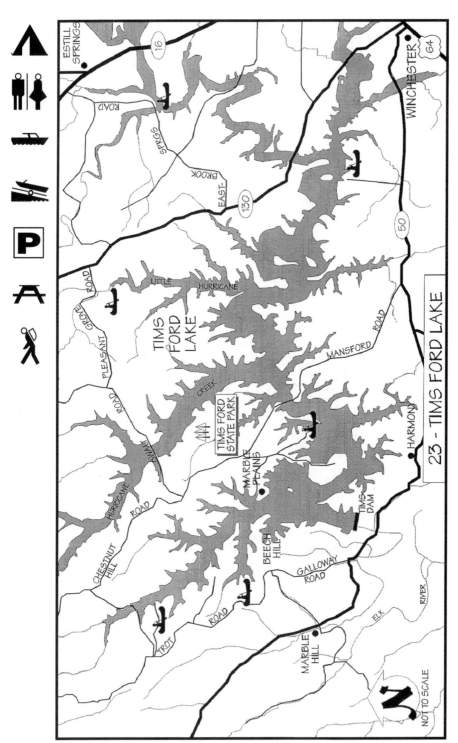

23 - TIMS FORD LAKE

NOT TO SCALE

23 Tim's Ford Lake

USGS Quadrangles: Lynchburg East, Tullahoma, Lois Belvidere, Winchester
Tennessee Atlas: Map 22

Size: 34 miles long, 10,700 acres
Closest Town: Winchester
County: Franklin, Moore
Best Time of Year: Year-round

Description: Located in the rolling hills of southern Middle Tennessee, Tim's Ford Lake is a great place to dip your paddle and explore the many hidden coves and long, winding creeks. The Tim's Ford area has a long history of good hunting and fishing. Archaeological excavations have uncovered numerous artifacts that indicate early Indian occupation as much as 12,000 years ago.

Like all TVA controlled reservoirs, the water level is lowered during the early fall, winter and spring months. Tim's Ford has a rather large draw-down of 23 feet. The full level is maintained from mid April through September. Although the lake is open for use Year-round, most prefer to visit it when water levels are up and the muddy shoreline is not exposed.

The nearby Tim's Ford State Park is a nice place to access the lake. However, some of the unimproved access points around the lake will be better for launching canoes during the busy summer season. The park has five miles of paved trails for cycling and beautiful lakeside cabins for rent from March 1 to December 1.

Directions: From Winchester, take Hwy 50 west. There are several access areas to the lake off of Hwy 50. To get to Tim's Ford State Park, continue on Hwy 50 west to Mansford Road turn-off on the right. After crossing Tim's Ford Lake on the causeway, take the first left into the state park.

Safety Considerations: BOAT TRAFFIC. AVOID WINDY CONDITIONS ON OPEN LAKE.
Ownership: Tennessee Valley Authority
Resource Numbers:
Tim's Ford State Park — 931/962-9184
1-800/471-5295

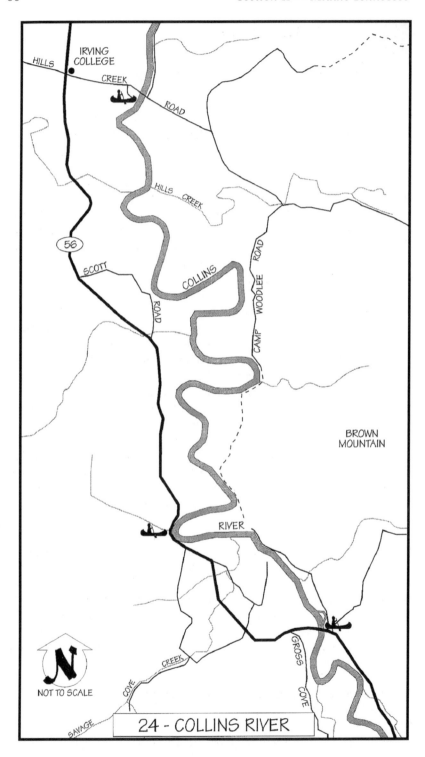

IRVING
COLLEGE

HILLS

CREEK

ROAD

HILLS CREEK

56

SCOTT

COLLINS

ROAD

CAMP WOODLEE ROAD

BROWN
MOUNTAIN

RIVER

GROSS

COVE

CREEK

COVE

NOT TO SCALE

SAVAGE

24 - COLLINS RIVER

Collins River

USGS Quadrangles: Altamont, Irving College
Tennessee Atlas: Map 39

Size: 9 river miles from Mt. Olive to Irving College
Closest Town: Irving College   **County:** Grundy, Warren
Best Time of Year: November through May. Check water levels.

Description: This section of the Collins River is a beautiful clear-water float that can only be paddled during high water levels in the winter and spring months. Since the Collins River is fed by springs and streams that run out of the pristine Savage Gulf complex, the water is incredibly luscious, with a blue-green hue where it flows over patches of white sandy bottom. Long, deep pools alternate with mild riffles. The river meanders past several small waterfalls cascading over moss-covered limestone bluffs.

Although the landscape around Irving College is dotted with large tree nurseries, the high banks keep the river secluded and quiet. The banks are either heavily forested with hardwoods and sycamores, or decorated with rock outcroppings that grow hemlocks and rhododendrons.

Those with "rock-hound" tendencies will particularly like the Collins, as it offers a wonderful selection of geodes, fossils and burnt-red rocks along portions of the river. The Collins has been declared a State Scenic River from the feeder spring known as Big Spring to the Hennessee Bridge. Fishing on the Collins River is considered good for rock bass, smallmouth bass, bluegill, trout and even muskie.

The minimum floatable level in this upper section is 1000 cubic feet per second (cfs) on the Collins gauge at McMinnville. To access this information, call the TVA Information Line at 1-800-238-2264. At the recording, push (3) to hear stream levels. Stay on the line for the Collins gauge reading at McMinnville.

Directions: From McMinnville, travel south on Hwy 56. From the intersection of Hwy 8, travel 14 miles to bridge over Collins River. Just after crossing the Collins River, immediately turn left onto paved road. A gravel road on the left leads to put-in under the bridge. The take-out is 8.6 miles north, under the bridge at Hills Creek Road. Another access point for a shorter run is off of Hwy 56 at a roadside park three miles north of the Collins River bridge, just on the county line between Warren and Grundy County.

Safety Considerations: DEADFALLS, STRAINERS.
Ownership: Private
Resource Numbers:
TVA Information Line — 1-800/238-2264

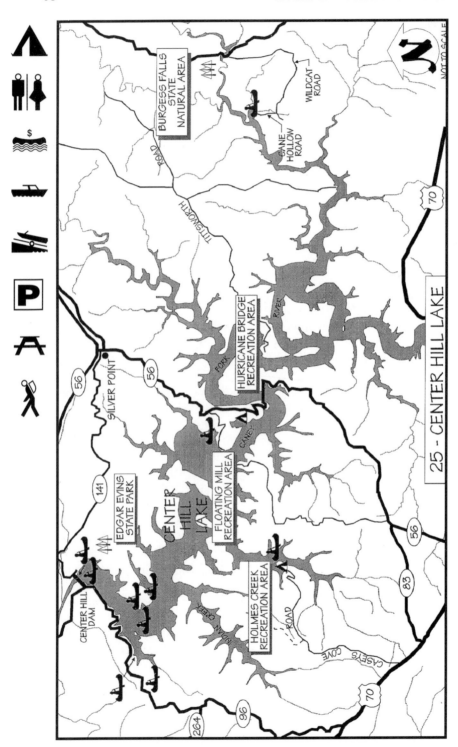

BURGESS FALLS
STATE
NATURAL AREA

WILDCAT
ROAD

CANE
HOLLOW
ROAD

TITSWORTH

ROAD

70

HURRICANE BRIDGE
RECREATION AREA

RIVER

FORK

25 - CENTER HILL LAKE

56

SILVER POINT

56

CANEY

FLOATING MILL
RECREATION AREA

141

EDGAR EVINS
STATE PARK

CENTER
HILL
LAKE

56

83

HOLMES CREEK
RECREATION AREA

CENTER HILL
DAM

INDIAN CREEK

ROAD

CASEYS COVE

70

264

96

NOT TO SCALE

25 Center Hill Lake

USGS Quadrangles: Center Hill Dam, Silver Point, Sligo Bridge
Tennessee Atlas: Map 39, 55, 56

Size: 64 miles long, 18,220 acres
Closest Town: Smithville   **County:** DeKalb, White, Warren
Best Time of Year: Year-round

Description: Center Hill Lake offers the canoer a large variety of options — from paddling the open areas of the scenic lake, to exploring any number of feeder creeks along its bank. With 18 launching ramps, seven marinas, nine recreation areas and three state parks located on Center Hill Lake, the hardest part is making a decision.

The main tributary into Center Hill Lake, the Upper Caney Fork River, has an interesting attraction for both paddlers and fisherman. Beneath the Great Falls Dam, in Rock Island State Rustic Park, there is a drop on the Caney Fork known as the Blue Hole. This deep pocket of water is just below a small series of falls and is nationally famous for its white bass and walleye spawning runs in the spring. Paddlers who want the thrill of a Class II-Class III run, through a short but fast series of rapids, often put in above this section at the end of the road (opposite the power plant) and run the large waves created by the dam which drop over several ledges before entering the Blue Hole. The less adventuresome option is to launch canoes below the Blue Hole, at the ramp next to the swimming beach at Rock Island State Rustic Park. From here you can paddle the slackwater leading up to the Blue Hole, or head out towards the main reservoir of Center Hill Lake. Rock Island has camping facilities and hiking trails along the edge of the Upper Caney Fork Rivers. There is a nice picnic area that overlooks the Blue Hole.

Rock Island is a spectacular place for watching a variety of wildlife and for viewing spring wildflowers. Yellow-crowned night herons are often spotted, as are white-tailed deer, wild turkey and even bats. Flying insects are abundant in the Caney Fork gorge during the summer, and naturally, so are the bats. At dusk the big brown bat and pipistrelle are seen out over the river.

Another fun area to explore around Center Hill Lake is the Burgess Falls State Natural Area. This little gem is located up another Center Hill Tributary, that is aptly named, Falling Water River. This river is easily accessible with several boat launch sites near its mouth, but the closest access to the falls is located off of Can Hol Road in White County. When putting in below the falls, it is a short 2.5 mile paddle up to the falls. You can paddle to within 100 yards of the falls, then take out and walk up to the base. During the early spring when the dogwoods are blooming, this is a spectacular sight. There is also a feeder creek, known as Cane Creek, that can be explored from the put-in on Falling Water River. A worthwhile side-trip is to hike the rim trails at Burgess Falls State Natural Area.

Directions: Center Hill Lake is only minutes away from Cookeville, Lebanon, Smithville, McMinnville, Sparta and Carthage, and an hour drive from Nashville on I-40 east.

    To Upper Caney Fork River and the Blue Hole at Rock Island State Park: From McMinnville, travel north on US 70 south. Take Hwy 1 north to Rock Island, then turn left on Rock Island-Green Hill Road towards the state park. Put-in at boat launch near the swimming beach.

    To put-in below Burgess Falls State Natural Area: From I-40 west of Cookeville, take exit 286 onto Hwy 135 south (Burgess Falls Road) Travel 8.5 miles to turn-off for Burgess Falls State Natural Area. Just past the park entrance, take a sharp left on Austin Road and go 2 miles to right turn on Browntown Road. Drive less than 1 mile and turn right on Wildcat Road, then 1 mile to right turn on Can Hol Road (a gravel road that runs through a small creek before the access area at the end of the road.)

Safety Considerations: BOAT TRAFFIC. AVOID WINDY CONDITIONS ON OPEN LAKE.
Ownership: U.S. Corps of Engineers
Resource Numbers:
    Resource Manager, Center Hill Lake — 615/548-4521
    Burgess Falls State Natural Area — 931/432-5312
    Rock Island State Park — 931/686-2471 or 1-800/713-6065
    Edgar Evins State Park — 1-800/250-8619

Burgess Falls State Natural Area is just a short canoe trip up Falling Water River, a tributary of Center Hill Lake.

26 Caney Fork River

USGS Quadrangles: Center Hill Dam, Buffalo Valley
Tennessee Atlas: Map 55

Size: 8.7 river miles from Center Hill Dam to Betty's Island
Closest Town: Buffalo Valley   **Counties:** Dekalb, Putnam, Smith
Best Time of Year: Year-round

Description: Just below the Center Hill Dam in northern De Kalb County, the Caney Fork River continues its flow towards the Cumberland River. Interestingly, this section of river is actually three different rivers, depending on the water level. When two generators are running, the water level will be eight feet higher than when no water is being released through the dam. Even though the river can be easily navigated when it runs at high levels, the faster flow will make it a quick trip down river. The higher water levels will also cover up many of the gravel bars and small islands that are abundant on the Caney Fork. When levels are low, these gravel bars make nice picnic areas and swimming spots. During the summer months the water is very clear, allowing an opportunity for underwater viewing with snorkel and mask.

This section of river below the dam is wide and twisted, making the trip a visual treat as one floats down past ancient limestone cliffs and low cultivated farmland. The wildlife is abundant and you may well catch a glimpse of a bald eagle during the winter months as they feed in the river. Other birds of prey such as the red-tailed hawk are common sights flying just over the tree-tops. During the fall and winter seasons, listen for the beautiful call of the loon.

The Caney Fork River has several good access points and an outfitter nearby who rents canoes. Located on Center Hill Lake, Edgar Evins State Park has nice camping facilities and miles of hiking trails. There are also some high islands in the river that are used for camping. Be sure never to set up camp below the high water line, since generating schedules can be less than reliable at times.

You may hear stories of fishermen who have to scramble up the banks of the river when the generators are turned on. This is no exaggeration - especially close to the dam. So, to avoid being taken by surprise when water levels rise quickly, be sure to call ahead for release schedules and for the number of generators in operation. The newly released water takes several hours to make it to the take-out, so if you want to run the river at a faster flow, you will need to wait at least two hours after generation commences to begin paddling. If you don't, you will actually outrun the rise in water, paddling into slower moving water as you head downstream.

To find out when water will be released, call the TVA Lake

Information Line at 1-800-238-2264. At the recording, press (4) to access the water release schedule. For Center Hill Dam, press (37). To find out the release schedule for the following day, press (#). You will want to be sure that at least one generator will be running during the time of your trip.

Directions: Exit off of I-40 at Buffalo Valley (exit 268) just west of Cookeville. Turn left onto Buffalo Valley Road (Rt. 96) and travel 4.7 miles to intersection of Hwy 141 at Laurel Hill. (Caney Fork Canoe Rentals will be on the right). Turn right on Hwy 141 and travel a short distance until the next right turn where a sign reads "Resource Manger/ Visitors Information." Drive past the manager's office to the boat launch area and parking lot at the end of the road.

Drive 8 miles to take-out at Betty's Island. The best way to find this access area is to turn right out of the parking area below the dam, go over the dam and take an immediate right onto Lancaster Highway. Go approximately 4 miles to a right turn onto Betty's Bend Road. Go over one-lane wooden-rail bridge to dead end on St. Mary's Road. Turn right on St. Mary's Road and immediately turn right into Betty's Bend access area. (Signs are frequently missing.)

Safety Considerations: WATER LEVELS RISE QUICKLY BELOW DAM.
Ownership: Tennessee Valley Authority (TVA)
Resource Numbers:
    TVA Lake Information Line — 1-800/238-2264
    Edgar Evins State Park — 1-800/250-8619
    Resource Manager Center Hill Lake — 615/548-4521
    Big Rock Canoe Rentals — 931/858-0967

High bluffs along the Caney Fork River are decorated with wildflowers and blooming dogwood trees in the spring months.

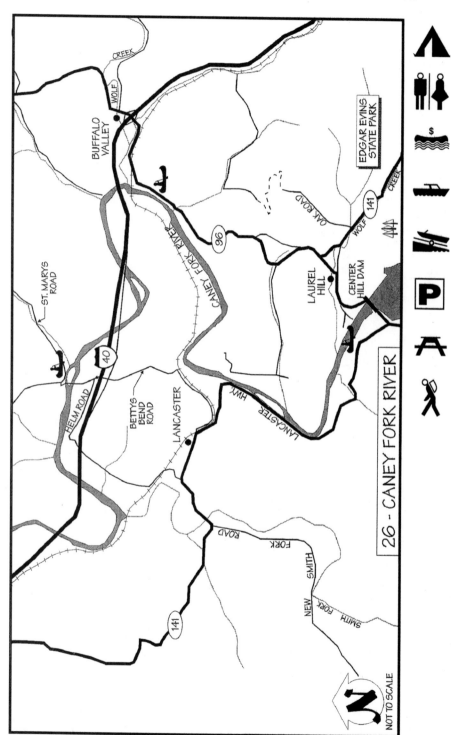

26 - CANEY FORK RIVER

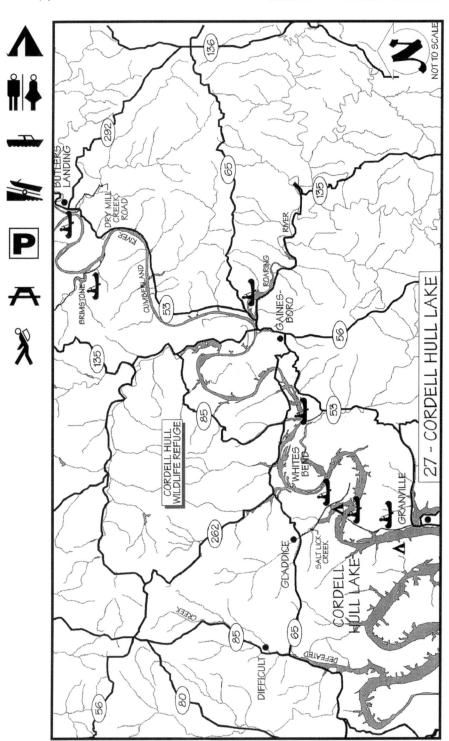

Cordell Hull Lake

USGS Quadrangles: Dale Hollow Dam, Celina, Burristown, Whitleyville, Gainesboro, Granville
Tennessee Atlas: Maps 66, 56, 55

Size: 53 river miles from Celina to Granville
Closest Town: Celina   **Counties:** Clay, Jackson
Best Time of Year: Year-round

Description: Cordell Hull Lake is one of the impoundments of the Cumberland River created in 1973 by the U.S. Corps of Engineers. This particular portion of the Cumberland River, although it is technically a 72-mile long dam controlled reservoir, retains much of its original qualities. Winding around the moderately mountainous terrain, Cordell Hull Lake is more like a large river than a lake. The quaint town of Granville is an old river town which once bustled with activity during the paddle-wheel era when river travel was the main mode of transportation for delivering materials to Nashville. During the month of September, a paddle-wheel boat operates on the Cumberland River from Nashville to Gainesboro. More information can be obtained about this historic journey through the Smith County Chamber of Commerce.

Cordell Hull Lake provides a long, serpentine canoe trail that will take the better part of a week to explore. Fortunately, with so many access areas along the way, it can easily be done in sections. The most scenic route is from Celina to Granville, which offers several recreation areas for camping, picnicking and hiking. Fort Blount historic site is along this section of river, as are extensive hiking trails that connect Holleman's Bend Recreation Area to Granville. There are fishing opportunities galore on Cordell Hull Lake. Anglers frequently catch largemouth bass, smallmouth bass, crappie, catfish, white bass, striped bass, sauger, trout and bream. They also occasionally catch the rare paddlefish which looks like a shovel-nosed catfish. Paddlefish are members of the ancient fish family *Polyodontidae*. They feed on tiny planktonic animals which are filtered through gill rakers. One of two surviving species lives in the USA — the other is found in China.

The lake was named after one of Tennessee's finest Volunteers — Cordell Hull. After he became known around the world for his role in creating the United Nations, Hull was awarded the Nobel Peace Prize in 1945. His birthplace is located east of Dale Hollow Lake near the town of Bloomington.

Directions: To access the boat launch at Donaldson Recreation Area in Celina, take I-40 to Hwy 56 north (exit 280). Just north of Gainesboro, turn right onto Hwy 53. Travel north on Hwy 53 to the junction of Hwy 52 west towards Celina. Go less than one mile to four-way stop. Turn right and then left just past garage. Travel just over one mile to entrance at Donaldson Recreation Area on right.

Safety Considerations: GUSTY WINDS. POWERBOAT TRAFFIC.
Ownership: U.S. Corps of Engineers
Resource Numbers:
   Resource Manager, Cordell Hull Lake — 615/735-1034
   Smith County Chamber of Commerce — 615/735-2093

The musical honking of large flocks af Canada geese is now a familiar sound along many rivers and lakes in Tennessee.

28 Roaring River

USGS Quadrangles: Dodson Branch, Whitleyville
Tennessee Atlas: Map 55, 56

Size: 11 river miles from Old Roaring River Road to U.S. Corps of Engineers boat ramp on the Cumberland River
Closest Town: Gainesboro   **County:** Jackson
Best Time of Year: Year-round from fish dam to Cumberland River, upper section winter and spring or after rain

Description: The Roaring River is a small, intimate stream that makes its way through Jackson county, where it joins the Cumberland River at the Cordell Hull Impoundment. The Roaring River and two of its tributaries, Spring Creek and Blackburn Fork, are designated state scenic rivers - and rightfully so, as they flow through shallow valleys and into deep, wooded gorges. As the name implies, there are sections of the Roaring River that are raging whitewater. These, however, are farther upstream in Overton County.

The lower part is an easy Class I stream that runs through a narrow farming valley, flanked by vertical rock walls. About halfway between the put-in and the fish barrier dam is an interesting site known as the "boils." This is an area where a spring flows with such force from under the riverbed that the water bubbles up as if it were boiling. A large gravel bar has formed around the boils that can be used for picnicking and even parking. This is also a good access area. The hillsides above the Roaring River are filled with wildflowers in the spring. Look for shooting stars, twin leaf, spiderwort and bloodroot.

The fish barrier dam must be portaged if traveling on down to the Cumberland River take-out. One way to recognize the fish barrier dam from upstream is by spotting the power lines that cross the river over the dam.

Although the upper section of Roaring River is the most scenic, there is not enough flow to canoe through the summer. The section from the put-in just after the Blackburn Fork confluence to the Cumberland River is good year-round.

Directions: From I-40, take Hwy 56 north (exit 280) towards Gainesboro and Dale Hollow Dam. Just past Gainesboro, take 53 north for less than 1 mile to Hwy 135 east. (At this point, Roaring River will be on the left.) The U.S. Corps of Engineers boat ramp is another .5 mile on the left. From the Corps boat ramp and parking area, proceed east on Hwy 135. At 3.5 miles turn left onto a gravel road for the fish barrier dam access. To put in above the fish barrier dam, travel another 3 miles to an access area on the left (just past the confluence of Blackburn Fork). Or travel 4 miles from the fish barrier dam to Overton Road on the left. Take Overton Road over the bridge, then turn right onto Old Roaring River Road. Travel another 5 miles to the public put-in on the right. On the Roaring River, the road miles are approximately the same as the river miles.

Safety Considerations: STRAINERS AND DEADFALLS. PORT-AGE FISH BARRIER DAM.
Ownership: Private along banks. U.S. Corps of Engineers at the Cumberland River access and at the fish barrier dam access.
Resource Numbers:
    U.S. Corps of Engineers — 615/736-7161

Red-shouldered hawks are large birds-of-prey that often hunt the wooded hillsides along the Roaring River. They have a distinctive two-syllable scream that sounds like "kee-yer, kee-yer."

The fish weir dam was built by TVA in order to keep stocked fish from travelling upstream. The dam has good access on both sides of the river and provides the best launching point during the summer and fall months when water levels upstream tend to be low.

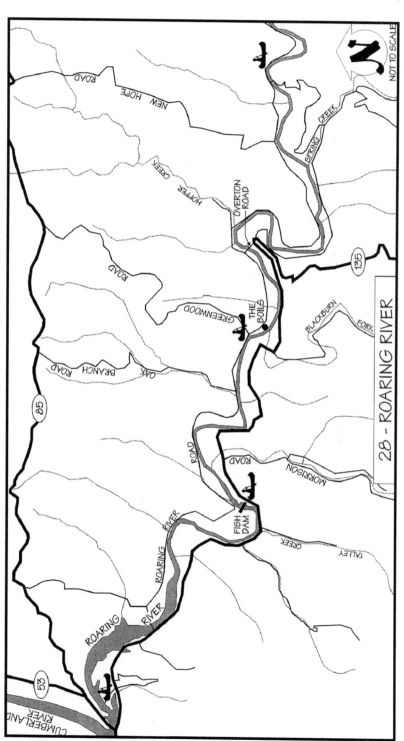

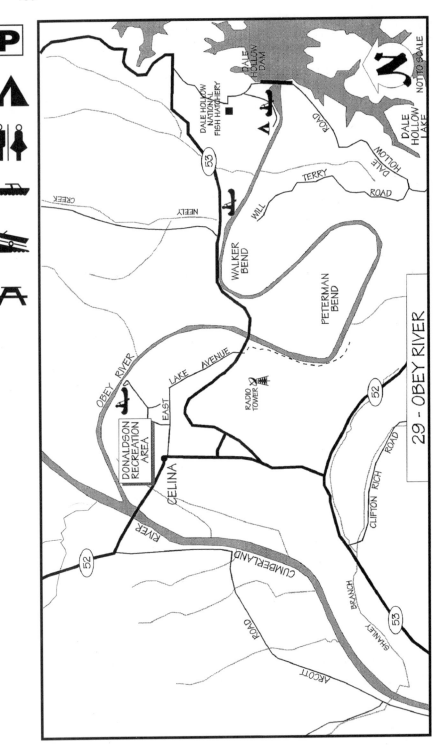

29 - OBEY RIVER

29 Obey River

USGS Quadrangles: Dale Hollow Dam, Celina
Tennessee Atlas: Map 66

Size: 6 river miles from Dale Hollow Dam to Celina
Closest Town: Celina   **County:** Clay
Best Time of Year: Year-round when dam is releasing

Description: The Obey River is the main feeder river into the Dale Hollow Lake reservoir, with only a small portion of it wandering from the Dale Hollow Dam to its mouth at the Cumberland River. This abbreviated, seven mile section below the dam provides a wonderful Class I canoe float when the dam is operating. The fishing is excellent in the Obey River below the dam and you can catch rainbow trout, bass, crappie, and bream. The scenery switches from massive limestone cliffs to low pastoral bottomlands. Bald eagles can be seen perched on snags along the banks of the Obey River during the winter months, usually from mid-December through mid-February. (There have also been sightings of the golden eagle, which is uncommon in Tennessee.) If you have the time, the Dale Hollow National Fish Hatchery is worth a visit. The public can tour the aquarium and small visitor center from 7am-4pm.

Most paddlers prefer to canoe when at least one generator is running, even though there is enough water to canoe when no generators are on. To find out when water will be released, call the TVA Lake Information Line at 1-800-238-2264. At the recording, press (4) to access the water release schedules. Then press (35) for Dale Hollow Dam. This will connect you to the dam release schedule for that day. To find out the release schedule for the following day, press (#).

Directions: From I-40, take Hwy 56 north (exit 280) towards Gainesboro and Dale Hollow Dam. Travel for 18.5 miles to Hwy 53 north. Turn right on Hwy 53 north and travel through Celina to turn off at Dale Hollow Dam Road. Boat launch is at the end of the road past the fish hatchery. Shuttle cars 4.5 miles to Donaldson Recreation Area in Celina. From the Dale Hollow Dam, turn left onto Hwy 53. Travel for 2.5 miles to right turn onto East Lake Avenue. Go 3.5 miles to right turn onto small unmarked road. Travel a short distance on this road to Donaldson Recreation Area boat launch.

Safety Considerations: BOAT TRAFFIC. WATER LEVELS CHANGE ABRUPTLY WHEN GENERATORS ARE TURNED ON.
Ownership: U. S. Corps of Engineers
Resource Numbers:
    Resource Manager, Dale Hollow Lake — 931/243/3136
    TVA information line — 1-800/238-2264

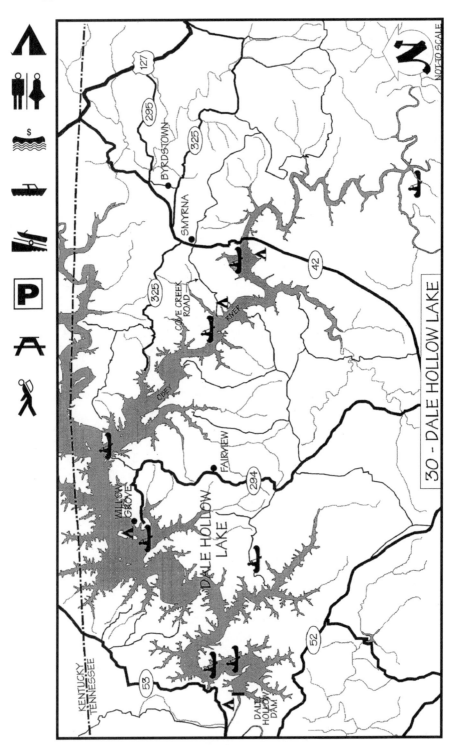

30 - DALE HOLLOW LAKE

Dale Hollow Lake Canoe Trail

USGS Quadrangles: Dale Hollow Dam, Dale Hollow Reservoir, Byrdstown
Tennessee Atlas: Map 66

Size: 61 miles long, 30,990 acres
Closest Town: Celina   **County:** Clay, Pickett
Best Time Of Year: Year-round

Description: Dale Hollow Lake is a Cumberland River impoundment that backs up into the Wolf River and the Obey River, where this trail begins. The U.S. Corps of Engineers has mapped out a 55-mile canoe trail that begins at Eastport Dock on the Obey River and ends at the Pleasant Grove Recreation Area — directly across from Dale Hollow Dam. The canoe trail passes many recreation areas where camping and picnicking are permitted. With numerous small islands, inlets, coves, and the forested Cumberland foothills rolling back from its shores, the irregularly-shaped lake is fun to explore by canoe. Motorboats are permitted, but paddlers can always find a secluded bay that no one else has discovered.

After passing through the steep slopes of the Obey River, the lake opens up, but still provides numerous coves and creeks. Because the lake is a highland reservoir with heavily wooded drainage basins, it lacks siltation, allowing the water to remain clear and clean. So clear is Dale Hollow Lake that it sports a fair number of scuba diving enthusiasts whose red and white flags dot the lake in summer months.

Wildlife is usually abundant on the lake, with ducks, deer, squirrel, muskrat and an occasional bald eagle being spotted. The fishing is rated as excellent, and Dale Hollow is noted worldwide for record-producing smallmouth bass. Upon completion of your canoe trip, be sure to stop in at the National Fish Hatchery where you can view hatchery fish in an aquarium at the visitor center.

Directions: The main highways leading north from I-40 to the area around Dale Hollow are, from east to west, TN 127 and TN 28 to Jamestown, TN 84 from Monterey to Livingston, TN 42 and TN 136 from Cookeville, TN 56 from Baxter, and TN 53 from the Gordonsville - Carthage exit.

Safety Considerations: AVOID WINDY CONDITIONS ON OPEN LAKE. BOAT TRAFFIC IS HEAVY IN SUMMER MONTHS.
Ownership: U.S. Corps of Engineers
Resource Numbers:
Resource Manager, Dale Hollow Lake — 931/243-3136

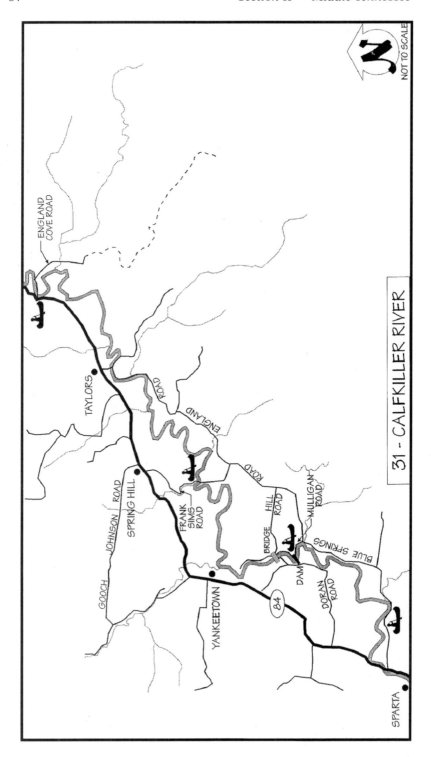

NOT TO SCALE

ENGLAND COVE ROAD

TAYLORS

ENGLAND ROAD

ROAD

SPRING HILL

JOHNSON ROAD

GOOCH

FRANK SIMS ROAD

YANKEETOWN

BRIDGE HILL ROAD

MULLIGAN ROAD

DAM

BLUE SPRINGS

DORAN ROAD

84

SPARTA

31 - CALFKILLER RIVER

③1 Calfkiller River

USGS Quadrangles: Monterey Lake, De Rossett
Tennessee Atlas: Map 56, 40

Size: 12 river miles from England Cove Bridge to Milligan Road
Closest Town: Sparta   **County:** White
Best Time of Year: Mid-December to Late April, or after heavy rainfall

Description: Despite its name, the upper section of the Calfkiller River is a docile Class I stream that wiggles its way through tree-lined banks and rocky bluffs. The narrow river has good access points and is surprisingly underused by paddlers. The Calfkiller can be quite snappy after a rain, and there is one Class II rapid just under the Frank Sims Road Bridge about halfway down this section of river. Just beyond this small rapid is a large deadfall that may need to be portaged.

Despite its close proximity to a heavily-populated area, the Calfkiller River provides a wonderful wildlife corridor. Canoeists often spot mink, river otter and a variety of birds including great horned owls, red-shouldered hawks and colorful wood ducks. The clear water provides a good view of life below the surface. Look for wildflowers such as Virginia bluebells and bloodroot in the spring, and beautiful foliage in the fall. Waterfalls that cascade down over moss-covered limestone ledges are a common sight along the Calfkiller.

A good indication of adequate water levels for running the Calfkiller is to observe the amount of water over the gravel bar at the put-in off England Cove Road. There should be at least six inches of water over the bar to canoe the Calfkiller. There is also a broken dam at the Milligan Road access point that should be portaged if paddling beyond this take-out. About fifteen miles below Sparta, the Calfkiller becomes one with the Caney Fork River.

Directions: From Interstate 40, east of Cookville, take US 70 N south towards Calfkiller. Travel approximately 7 miles south on US 70 N to Mill Creek Road (mile marker 4). Turn right on Mill Creek Rd and continue for 4.2 miles till it dead ends on Hwy 84. Turn right and travel for 4.4 miles to England Cove Road (just after crossing the county line into White County). Turn left onto gravel area next to England Cove Road. Launch canoes under the England Cove Bridge.

Shuttle cars to Milligan Road take-out by traveling 6 miles south on Hwy 84 to left hand turn on Doran Rd. Travel less than 1 mile to left-hand turn onto bridge over the Calfkiller. Just over the bridge, turn right onto Milligan Rd. Continue for .5 miles to gravel parking area on right side of road at site of broken dam.

For a shorter river trip, access the Calfkiller River at Frank Sims Road, which is 4 miles beyond England Cove Road on Hwy 84. The put-in is before crossing the bridge on the left side of the road. Be sure not to park in the private driveway that runs next to this access area. The river distance from Frank Sims Road to Milligan Road take-out is 4 miles.

Safety Considerations: WATCH FOR DEADFALLS AND STRAIN-ERS. RIVER BANKS ARE PRIVATELY OWNED. IF RUNNING BELOW MILLIGAN ROAD TAKE-OUT, PORTAGE AT BROKEN DAM.
Ownership: Private property along river banks

Except for a short, Class II rapid at the Frank Sims Road put-in, the Calfkiller River meanders slowly past wooded banks and towering limestone bluffs.

On a cloudy day or just around dusk, great horned owls are on the prowl. They can be seen gliding through the tree tops on large, silent wings as they scan the forest floor for small mammals.

32 Sequatchie River

USGS Quadrangles: Daus
Tennessee Atlas: Map 24

Size: 9 river miles from Hwy 127 to Condra Switch Road
Closest Town: Dunlap   **County:** Sequatchie
Best Time of Year: November through July

Description: The rugged mountains of the Southern Cumberland Plateau loom in the background of the beautiful Sequatchie River. Local outfitters like to refer to the scenic Class I stream as offering "gentle thrills" to those that venture onto the rural river. Whether one is after thrills or relaxation, this tranquil setting will provide a quality outdoor experience.

The Sequatchie Valley is a rift valley that was formed between two parallel geological faults. The mountains of the Cumberland Plateau on the east and the steep slopes of Walden Ridge on the left, tower 1300 feet above the valley floor. So unique is this type of formation that Sequatchie Valley is only one of two rift valleys in the world. The water that creates the Sequatchie River begins its flow in the northern Cumberland Plateau at Grassy Cove. But before it begins its descent down the valley, the Sequatchie River must travel four miles underground to avoid being blocked by the high walls of Bear Den Mountain. Many small springs emerge from the mountainside near the hamlet of Big Lick — forming the clear, cold headwaters of the Sequatchie River.

This is a highly recommended trip due to the unspoiled beauty of the Sequatchie Valley. Although there are over 70 canoeable miles on this meandering stream, all with good access and plenty of beautiful scenery, the area detailed is one of the most popular sections of the Sequatchie River. The depth of the river ranges from two to six feet, with an easy, yet steady, flow — making it fun, yet non-threatening. The nearby town of Dunlap is known for the numerous coke ovens built there in the early 1900's. Now on the National Historic Register, the ruins of these coke ovens can be seen standing in rows in the forest at the Coke Ovens Park in Dunlap. Another historic landmark along the Sequatchie River is Ketner Mill, located east of Victoria. The tall, red-brick structure was originally built in 1824 by David Ketner. Although it stopped operating in 1994, it is still owned by the Ketner family and remains in good condition.

The local outfitters in Dunlap are very knowledgeable about river conditions after periods of heavy rain. They are also willing to provide shuttle service for private boaters.

Directions: From Interstate 27 north of Chattanooga, take Hwy 127 north towards Dunlap. One mile past the junction of Hwy 283, Hwy 127 will cross the Sequatchie River. Turn right just over the bridge to access the river. To shuttle cars to take-out, travel back to Hwy 283 and turn right. Travel for 5.5 miles to right turn onto Condra Switch Road. Travel 1.6 miles to access area on left before crossing the Sequatchie River.

For a shorter float trip, take-out at the Tate Road Bridge.

Safety Considerations: DEADFALLS AND STRAINERS. FLASH-FLOODING AFTER HEAVY RAINS.
Ownership: Private
Resource Numbers:
Canoe the Sequatchie Canoe Rental — 423/949-4400

Despite its narrow channel and abundant gravel bars, the Sequatchie River is a year-round float stream.

Long lines of stone coke ovens are still standing at the Coke Oven Historic Site near the Sequatchie River in the small town of Dunlap.

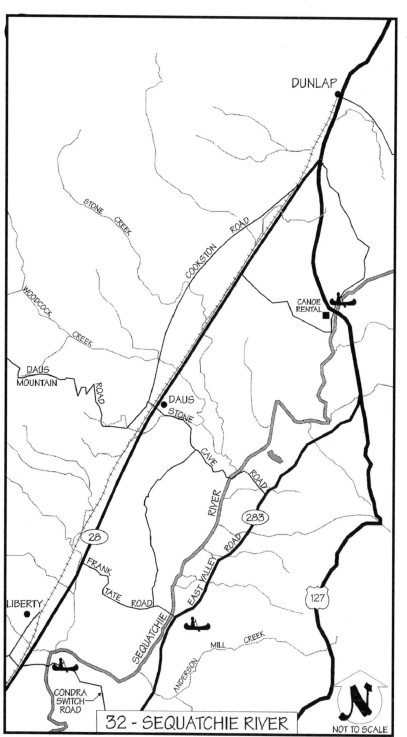

DUNLAP

STONE CREEK ROAD

COOKSTON ROAD

WOODCOCK

CREEK

CANOE RENTAL

DAUS MOUNTAIN

ROAD

DAUS STONE

CAVE ROAD

RIVER ROAD

283

28

EAST VALLEY ROAD

FRANK TATE ROAD

LIBERTY

SEQUATCHIE

127

MILL CREEK

ANDERSON

CONDRA SWITCH ROAD

32 - SEQUATCHIE RIVER

N

NOT TO SCALE

Section III

East Tennessee

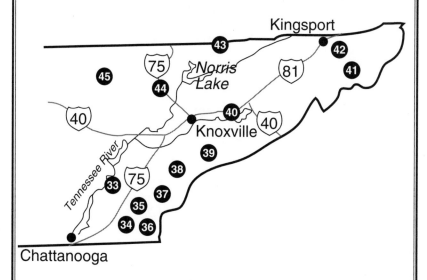

Kingsport

43

Norris Lake

75

81

45

44

42

41

40

40

Knoxville

40

39

Tennessee River

38

33

75

37

35

34

36

Chattanooga

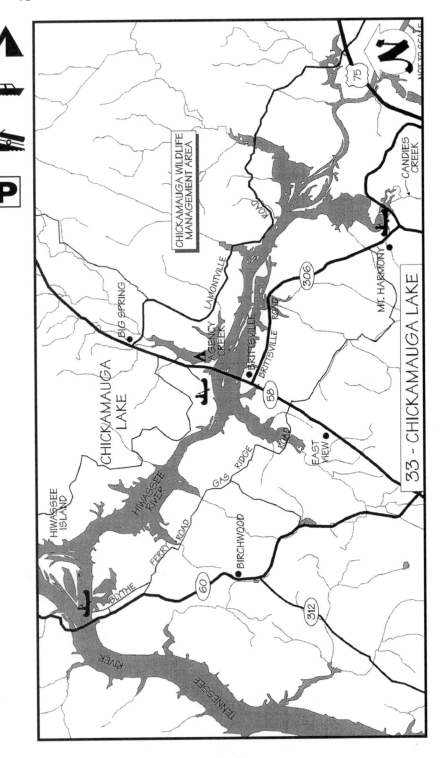

33 Chickamauga Lake

USGS Quadrangles: Big Spring, Birchwood, Graysville
Tennessee Atlas: Map 25

Size: NA
Closest Town: Dayton   **County:** Meigs
Best Time of Year: Year-round

Description: Although there are thousands of miles of shoreline on Chickamauga Lake and numerous access areas on this large impoundment of the Tennessee River, the marshy wetland area where the Hiwassee River meets the Tennessee River is an exciting wildlife viewing area and a peaceful part of the lake to explore by canoe. This section of the lake is within the Hiwassee Wildlife Refuge. Be aware that certain areas around the refuge are open only to hunters during limited small and big game seasons. Expect the lake levels to be low from late fall to early spring

Various mudflats, croplands and marshy ponds in the Hiwassee Wildlife Refuge provide habitat for a great variety of waterfowl. This is also the area most likely to see large flocks of sandhill cranes as they migrate between breeding grounds in the remote Arctic and wintering grounds in Florida. From November through late March, up to 5,000 of these majestic, slate-grey birds rest and feed in this area of Chickamauga Lake. Look for them feeding on Hiwassee Island or in nearby corn fields. Wildlife managers ask that you observe them from a distance. Even if you don't catch a glimpse of these large cranes, their trumpeting call which sounds like a loud "kar-r-r-o-o-o" is an experience you will never forget.

Directions: There are two good launch points into the Chickamauga Lake at the Hiwassee Wildlife Refuge. One is the Old Blythe Ferry terminal off of Hwy 60. From the junction of Hwy 58 and Hwy 60 near Georgetown, follow Hwy 60 for 7.8 miles north. Turn right onto Meigs County Road 131, and then fork left onto Blythe Ferry Road. Travel less than one mile to the old ferry terminal.

Another Tennessee Wildlife Resources Agency (TWRA) managed launch is located off of Hwy 58 just after crossing the Hiwassee River Bridge. Look for a small gravel road on the northwest side of the bridge. Road may be muddy, and there is no sign to the turn-off. Across the road from this turn-off is the Agency Creek Campground, managed by the TWRA.

Safety Considerations: AVOID WINDY CONDITIONS ON OPEN LAKE. BOAT TRAFFIC WILL BE HEAVY IN SUMMER MONTHS.
Ownership: Tennessee Valley Authority
Resource Numbers:
Tennessee Wildlife Resource Agency — 1-800-262-6704

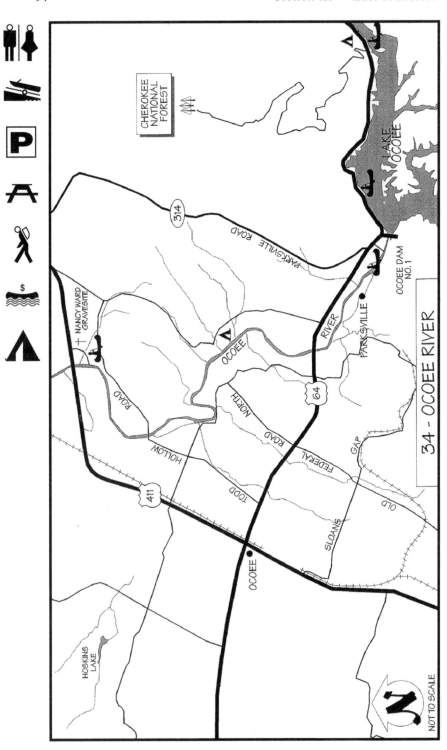

34 - OCOEE RIVER

34 Ocoee River

USGS Quadrangles: Parksville, Benton
Tennessee Atlas: Map 26

Size: 7.5 miles from Ocoee Dam No.1 to US 411 access at Nancy Ward Gravesite
Closest Town: Parksville   **County:** Polk
Best Time of Year: Year-round when generators are running

Description: Spectacular and awesome — that's the Ocoee. Famous for its raging white-water upper section, the Ocoee was the site for the 1996 Olympic whitewater canoe and kayak events. Although still beautiful and rugged, the lower sections of the Ocoee are a much tamer form of the Olympic venue. In fact, there are four separate impoundments of the Ocoee River, including Lake Ocoee, that offer very different paddling experiences. The first two sections are steep and fast. This is the area where whitewater rafting and canoeing is at its best. Then, below Ocoee Powerhouse No. 2, the river backs up into Lake Ocoee — also known as Parksville Lake. The lake is a favorite spot for fishermen and speed boaters alike. In the off season it is a wonderful playground for open canoes. There are several access points around the lake and a large island not too far from shore where camping and picnicking activities are popular. Nestled between the steep slopes of Sugar Loaf and Bean Mountains, in the heart of the Cherokee National Forest, Lake Ocoee is postcard picture perfect.

The next section of the Ocoee River lies just on the other side of the Parksville Dam and is controlled by the water release schedule from Ocoee Dam No. 1. Since there are five generators that are operated from this dam, the water level will fluctuate a great deal according to the generation schedule. The TVA Information Line is reached by calling 1-800-238-2264. When the recording comes on, press (4) to access the water release schedule, then press (26) for Ocoee Dam No. 1. To find out the release schedule for the following day, press the (#) button. For a fast float trip in this section, there should be two or more generators running. With all five generators running, the river will be too fast for novice open-boat paddlers, and with no generators it will be very rocky and extremely slow. Be sure to call ahead or look at river flow before putting in. An alternate trip if the water flow is too swift is the nearby Hiwassee River.

There is a TVA park located at the put-in below Ocoee Dam No 1. Here visitors can view a one-tenth scale model of the Olympic whitewater course. The 300 foot long, 30 foot wide model allowed course designers to predict flow patterns, wave height, flow velocity, and water depth for the actual coarse. The park has visual exhibits about the building of the Olympic course as well as historical information on the Ocoee No. 1

Powerhouse. Once called the "Dynamo of Dixie," this powerhouse was Tennessee's first large hydroelectric plant. Early photographs dating back to 1910 show the construction of the original dam and powerhouse.

Directions: From Cleveland, Tennessee, take US 64 east towards Ocoee. From the junction of US 411, continue on US 64 for 5 miles to Ocoee Dam No.1 on the right. Turn in just before the TVA and TODA offices. Shuttle cars to take-out down river near the US 411 bridge. Take US 64 west to US 411, turn right and go 3.5 miles to the state park launch area located at the Nancy Ward Gravesite.

Safety Considerations: WATER LEVELS CHANGE ABRUPTLY WHEN GENERATORS ARE TURNED ON.
Ownership: Tennessee Valley Authority
Resource Numbers:

TVA Information Line —
1-800/238-2264
Hiwassee/Ocoee State Scenic
Rivers — 423/263-0050
Ocoee Ranger District —
423/476-9700
Adventures Unlimited —
1-800/662-0667

The Ocoee River is famous for its raging whitewater, which is located along the upper reaches of the river. This is where the Canoe & Kayak Whitewater Slalom events were held during the 1996 Olympics.

Sugarloaf Mountain Park, located below the Parksville Dam, is a convenient place where canoers can launch their boats for a more peaceful float down the Ocoee River. Just above the dam is Lake Ocoee, another great destination for water sport enthusiasts.

㉟ Hiwassee River

USGS Quadrangles: Oswald Dome, Benton
Tennessee Atlas: Map 26

Size: 8 miles from US 411 to Old Patty Road access
Closest Town: Etowa   **County:** Polk
Best Time of Year: Year-round when generators are running

Description: It just doesn't get much prettier than this. The Hiwassee is a gorgeous river system worthy of its designation as a State Scenic River. The most famous float section is the upper section just below the Apalachia Powerhouse. However, this is rated as a Class II section that should not be paddled by beginners in open canoes. If you wish to experience this lovely part of the river, do it first in a rubber kayak that you can rent in Reliance or hook up with an experienced paddle group. The Tennessee Scenic Rivers Association offers classes in solo and tandem whitewater paddling on this section of the Hiwassee in the summer.

There is a slower section of the Hiwassee River that is perfect for a leisurely family float. This Class I section begins at the US 411 bridge and runs for eight miles through forested hillsides and some cultivated farmland. It is used a lot by fishermen — the Hiwassee is an excellent trout stream. There are plenty of places to camp in this region of the Cherokee National Forest. The closest place to the Hiwassee is the Gee Creek campground. In fact, this campground has an access area at Gee Creek, which enters the Hiwassee River just above the US 411 bridge.

The reason the Hiwassee is designated a State Scenic River is twofold: not only does it have clear, clean running water that supports habitat for more than 65 species of fish and several endangered mussels, but it also lies within a 750,000-acre forested watershed that is alive with wildlife activity. Look for mink, beaver, raccoon, osprey, great blue herons and North America's largest salamander — the hellbender. The John Muir National Recreation Trail begins in Reliance and meanders alongside the Hiwassee River for over 12 miles. Use caution along this trail in the summer when poisonous copperhead snakes may be basking along the riverbank.

Since this is a dam controlled river, always check water levels before planning a canoe trip. Call the TVA Information Line at 1-800/238-2264. When the recording comes on, press (4) to access the water release schedule, then press (22) for the Apalachia Dam. To find out the release schedule for the following day, press the (#) button. This section of the river should be paddled when one or two generators are running.

Directions: From Etowa, travel 6 miles south on US 411 to Hiwassee River Bridge. The State Park office is located across US 411 from the launch area. To shuttle cars to take-out, travel north on US 411 to Hwy 163 west. Travel for 3.7 miles to left turn on Old Patty Road in Dentville. Drive 6 miles, cross the Hiwassee Bridge, turn left onto gravel road leading to launch ramp.

Safety Considerations: WATER LEVELS CHANGE ABRUPTLY WHEN GENERATORS ARE TURNED ON. POISONOUS COPPERHEAD SNAKES ABUNDANT ON STREAM BANKS IN SUMMER.

Ownership: Tennessee Department of Environment and Conservation/ US Forest Service

Resource Numbers:

    Hiwassee River State Park — 423/263-0050

    U.S. Forest Service — 423/263-5486

    Webb Brothers Raft Rental — 423/338-2373

    Tennessee Scenic Rivers Association —

        P.O. Box 159041, Nashville, TN 37215

Fishing is a popular sport on the Hiwassee River. The cold mountain water that runs under the dam provides the ideal climate for rainbow trout.

Canoers on the upper section of the Hiwassee River often paddle whitewater canoes and wear extra safety equipment.

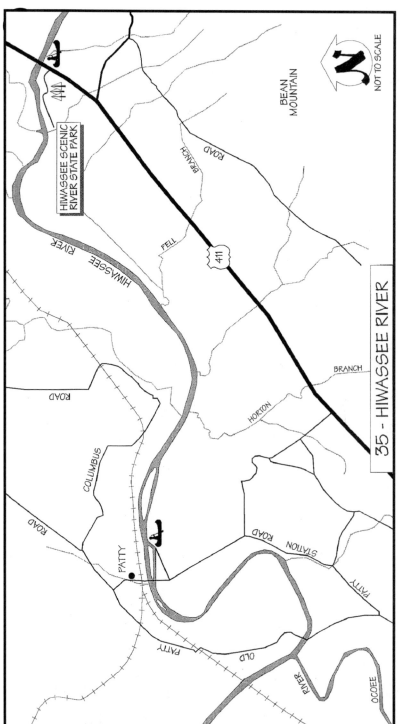

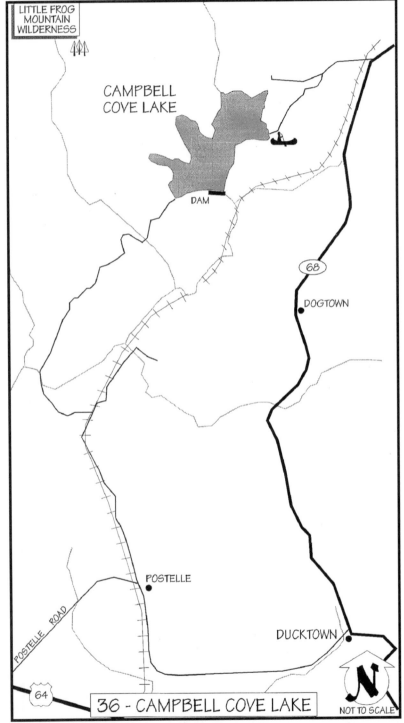

LITTLE FROG
MOUNTAIN
WILDERNESS

CAMPBELL
COVE LAKE

DAM

68

DOGTOWN

POSTELLE

POSTELLE ROAD

DUCKTOWN

64

36 - CAMPBELL COVE LAKE

N

NOT TO SCALE

36 Campbell Cove Lake

USGS Quadrangles: Ducktown
Tennessee Atlas: Map 26

Size: 89 acres
Closest Town: Ducktown   **County:** Polk
Best Time of Year: Year-round

Description: Small, but pretty, Campbell Cove Lake is hidden below the peaks of the Little Frog Mountain Wilderness Area. Gasoline-powered motors are not allowed on the lake, creating a tranquil atmosphere that is perfect for canoe exploration. Despite the fact that the lake is beginning to show signs of development along its shores where lots have been sold for lake side homes, there is a public access area and several sections around the perimeter that have remained undisturbed. Bass and catfish fishing are excellent on Campbell Cove Lake. No camping is allowed along the shores, but small cabins can be rented on the lake.

Directions: Located on Hwy 68, just north of US 64 in Ducktown. Turn left at Campbell Cove lake sign and stay on the main road for less than one mile. Public launch area will be on the left.

Safety Considerations: AVOID WINDY CONDITIONS ON OPEN LAKE.
Ownership: Private
Resource Numbers:
    Hideaway Cabins at Campbell Cove Lake — 1-800/390-8888

Always an exciting find, loons can be found in fall and winter. Listen for their eerie call around dusk.

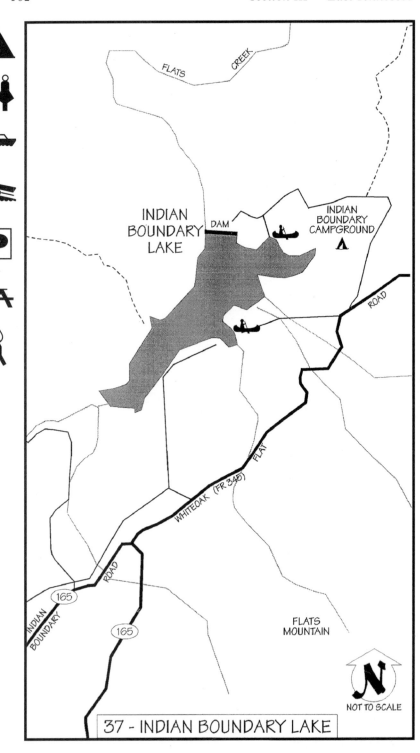

FLATS CREEK

INDIAN BOUNDARY LAKE

DAM

INDIAN BOUNDARY CAMPGROUND

ROAD

WHITEOAK (FR 345) FLAT

INDIAN BOUNDARY ROAD

165

165

FLATS MOUNTAIN

N

NOT TO SCALE

37 - INDIAN BOUNDARY LAKE

Indian Boundary Lake

USGS Quadrangles: Whiteoak Flats
Tennessee Atlas: Map 27

Size: 96 Acres
Closest Town: Tellico Plains   **County:** Monroe
Best Time of Year: Mid-April through October

Description: Indian Boundary Lake is an excellent recreation area for canoers as well as hikers, mountain bikers and those who just like to take in the scenery from the car. The drive up to Indian Boundary Lake winds along the Tellico River before branching off into the Turkey Creek Mountains. The lake is considered an excellent fishing reservoir, with only electric trolling motors and non-powered vessels permitted.

Located in the Cherokee National Forest, Indian Boundary Lake is secluded and peaceful. With a black bear sanctuary nearby and acres of undeveloped wilderness all around the lake, this is an excellent place to catch a glimpse of a black bear or maybe even the introduced European boar. Red squirrels, eastern chipmunks and fox are also residents in the lake region.

The facilities at Indian Boundary Lake were built in the 1930's by the Civilian Conservation Corps. The rustic park includes a campground, swimming beach, a boat ramp, and restrooms. There is also a small amphitheater where outdoor programs are conducted in season. Miles of foot paths and biking trails begin at the lake and wind up into the mountains overlooking Indian Boundary Lake and the nearby Citgo Creek Wilderness.

Directions: Take Hwy 165 east from Tellico Plains. Travel 13.7 miles on Hwy 165 (Indian Boundary Road) to left turn on National Forest Road 345. Go 1.5 miles and turn left into recreation area.

Safety Considerations: AVOID WINDY CONDITIONS ON OPEN LAKE.
Ownership: US Forest Service
Resource Numbers:
    US Forest Service — 423/253-2520

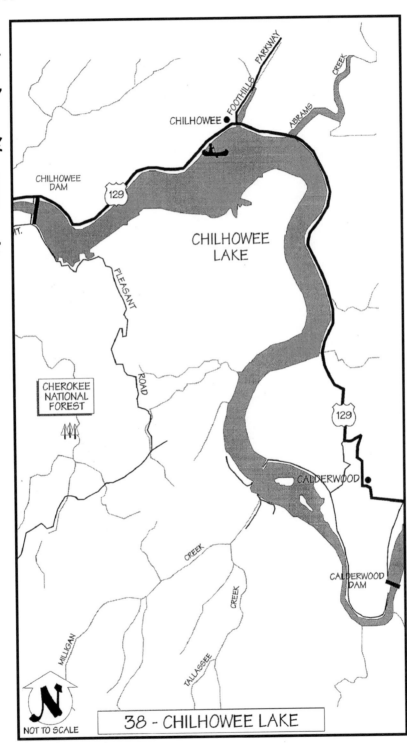

CHILHOWEE

CHILHOWEE
DAM

129

CHILHOWEE
LAKE

PLEASANT

ROAD

CHEROKEE
NATIONAL
FOREST

FOOTHILLS PARKWAY

CREEK

ABRAMS

129

CALDERWOOD

CREEK

CREEK

CALDERWOOD
DAM

MILLIGAN

TALLASSEE

N

NOT TO SCALE

38 - CHILHOWEE LAKE

38 Chilhowee Lake

USGS Quadrangles: Tallassee, Calderwood, Tapoco
Tennessee Atlas: Map 43, 27

Size: N/A
Closest Town: Tallassee **County:** Monroe, Blount
Best Time of Year: Year-round

Description: Chilhowee is one of the many lakes of the Little Tennessee River created over the last several decades as the TVA-built dams on all the major river systems across the state. Fortunately for paddlers and fishermen, not all of the lakes are huge inland seas, where water skiers and large motor boats rule the water. Lake Chilhowee is more like a river - narrow and twisted, it flows through both the Great Smoky Mountains National Park and the Cherokee National Forest. The access to Lake Chilhowee is easy and convenient, with several boat ramps located on US 129 along the northern border of the lake.

One nice place to explore is the opening into Abrams Creek which runs down out of the Great Smoky Mountains. This beautiful little feeder stream can be explored for quite a distance until the current becomes too great to paddle against. Or, paddlers may choose to put in on the next impoundment "upriver" from Chilhowee — Little Calderwood Lake. This section of the river crosses the state line into North Carolina. Because the two states could not decide who would claim rights to the recreational fishing on Calderwood Lake, anyone angling in these waters must have in their possession both a Tennessee and North Carolina fishing license.

All of the lakes of the Little Tennessee River provide excellent habitat for wintering waterfowl. The more common species are Canada geese, mallards, loons and widgeons.

Directions: Take 411 south from Knoxville, turn left on Hwy 72. Travel 9.3 miles and turn right on 129 south. Go 2 miles to TRDA boat access on right. There are several other access areas along Hwy 129. Camping is permitted along the highway at a number of small picnic areas.

Safety Considerations: AVOID WINDY CONDITIONS ON LAKE.

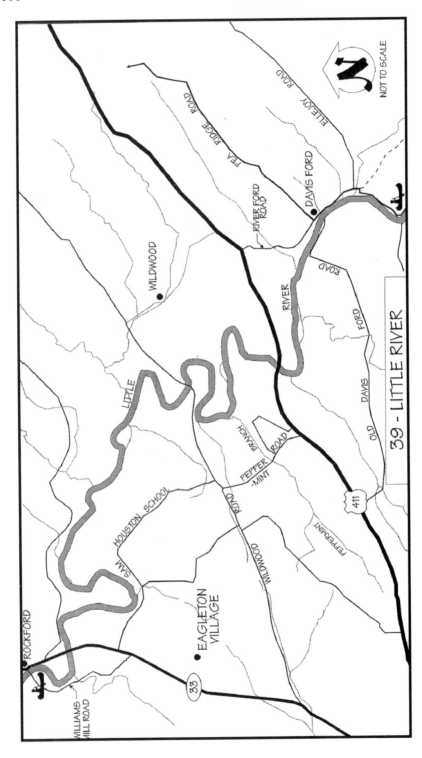

NOT TO SCALE

39 - LITTLE RIVER

39 Little River

USGS Quadrangles: Kinzel Springs, Wildwood, Maryville
Tennessee Atlas: Map 44, 43

Size: 12 river miles from Old Walland Hwy to Hwy 33 bridge
Closest Town: Maryville   **County:** Blount
Best Time of Year: December to late April

Description: Located just at the edge of the Great Smokey Mountains National Park, this section of the Little River is a quiet, yet snappy float stream. In its beginning, as it runs from the northwest side of Clingman's Dome, the Little River rushes through deep gorges and treacherous mountain terrain, where it is considered one of the most difficult white-water rivers in Tennessee. However, as it approaches Walland and beyond, the gradient flattens out and the river becomes a more leisurely Class I stream. The best access to the Little River for an easy float is just beyond the Melrose Dam at the Old Walland Highway bridge. Unfortunately, the next access point is quite a way down river at the Hwy 33 bridge.

Although there is a lot of development beginning to occur around the town of Maryville, this river is extremely scenic with tall, wooded hillsides and occasional limestone bluffs separating the encroaching city from the beauty of the little stream. Cultivated fields and pastures create some spectacular vistas and some interesting homes occasionally dot the river-bank. Dive bombing kingfishers, great blue herons and the occasional red-tailed hawk can be viewed overhead. This section of river is also a great fishing spot for trout and bass, so expect to be joined by local fishermen. Eventually, the river empties out into the Tennessee River near Singleton.

Directions: From Maryville, take US 411 east towards Sevierville. Take the first right onto River Ford Road after crossing the bridge over the Little River. Travel for 1.6 miles on River Ford Road to Ellejoy Road. Turn right and travel less than one mile to the access area before crossing bridge. To shuttle cars to the take-out, travel back to US 411 and turn left towards Maryville. Go 2.3 miles to right turn on Peppermint Road. (Do not turn on Peppermint Hills Road.) Travel for 1.1 miles and turn right at Wildwood Road. Immediately turn left onto Sam Houston School Road and drive to the Junction of Hwy 33. Turn right on Hwy 33 and go one mile to left turn on Williams Mill Road. Just over bridge, turn left into ball fields. Drive through fields to launch area under bridge.

Safety Considerations: STRAINERS AND DEADFALLS.
Ownership: Private

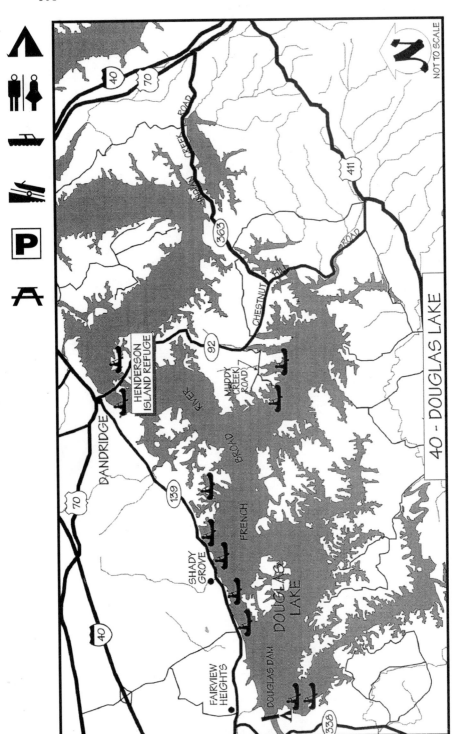

NOT TO SCALE

40 - DOUGLAS LAKE

40 Douglas Lake

USGS Quadrangles: Jefferson City, Shady Grove, Chestnut Hill, White Pine
Tennessee Atlas: Map 61, 45

Size: 30,400 acres
Closest Town: Dandridge   **County:** Jefferson
Best Time of Year: Year-round

Description: Douglas Lake is an expansive reservoir created at the confluence of its two major tributaries: the French Broad and the Nolichucky Rivers. Because of its unlimited coves and islands, Douglas Lake is a great canoe destination. Even during the busy summer months, paddlers can always find a secluded area away from powerboats.

Although there are many boat ramps for accessing the lake, a good place to begin your trip is right in the beautiful little town of Dandridge. There is a launch area on Hwy 139 in Shady Grove or across Hwy 92 bridge at the Dandridge Municipal Park. Another good access area for canoers is in Leadvale with access to the Rankin Wildlife Management Area. A lakeside campground is located between these two access areas in the small community of Oak Grove.

Douglas Lake provides endless enjoyment to the wildlife watcher at most any time of year. See bald eagles and short-eared owls in the winter and spectacular shorebirds in the fall. In the late summer watch for great egrets, little blue heron and black-crowned night herons. Spring is the time to catch nesting songbirds such as the common yellowthroat and red-winged blackbirds.

Directions: From Dandridge, take Hwy 92 south over bridge to launch areas. Or travel east on Hwy 9 to campground and boat ramp in Oak Grove. To access the Rankin Wildlife Management Area, take Hwy 113 north from I-40 west of Dandridge. Travel for 2.5 miles to right turn on Leadvale Road. Take Leadvale Road to Bridge access.

Safety Considerations: AVOID WINDY CONDITIONS ON OPEN LAKE. POWERBOAT TRAFFIC MAY BE HEAVY IN SUMMER MONTHS.
Ownership: Tennessee Valley Authority
Resource Numbers:
     Rankin Wildlife Management Area — 423/587-5600
     Dandridge Chamber of Commerce — 865/397-9642

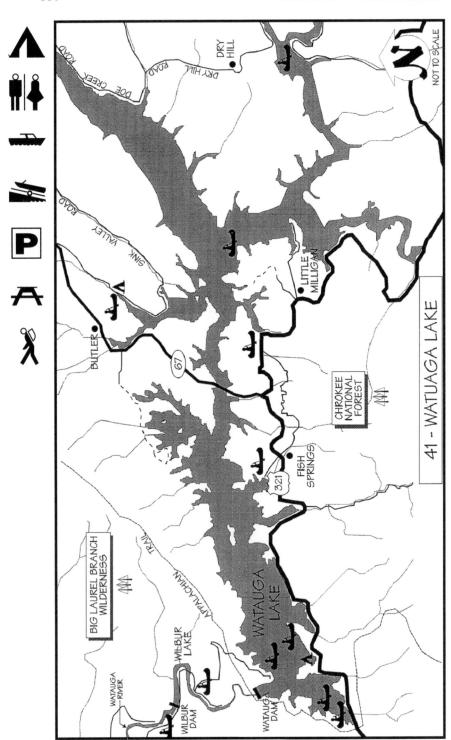

41 - WATUAGA LAKE

Watauga Lake

USGS Quadrangles: Watauga Dam, Elk Mills
Tennessee Atlas: Map 63, 46

Size: 16 miles long, 6,300 acres
Closest Town: Hampton   **County:** Carter, Johnson
Best Time of Year: Year-round

Description: Tucked away in the northeastern reaches of the Volunteer State, this beautiful mountain lake is reminiscent of days gone by, when only Cherokee Indians, fur traders, and a few pioneer settlers inhabited the area. With only one small marina on the lake and plenty of wilderness protecting the shores, Watauga is a special place. Along the entire northern shore, the Iron Mountains rise above the lake, creating a spectacular view from the Appalachian National Scenic Trail that runs along its ridge. On the southern side is Pond Mountain Wilderness and to the east are the Stone Mountains and the Pisgah National Forest in North Carolina.

The lake has several boat ramps along US 321, the only main road that runs along the southern shore. There are two campgrounds on the lake and several islands that are suitable for over-nights. Several unique waterfowl frequent Watauga lake and the lower impoundment known as Wilbur Lake. They include the oldsquaw and surf scoter. The deeper water attracts diving ducks such as the ring-necked duck and bufflehead — commonly seen in winter and spring months. The Watauga Dam is somewhat of an impressive sight — it is the highest dam in Tennessee, towering 331 feet above the river.

The Watauga River that runs below Wilbur Dam spills down through a spectacular gorge with beautiful rocky walls and wooded hillsides. This is a noted whitewater rafting run when the generators are running, as well as a superb trout fishing stream. When the generators are not running on the Watauga River, there is still enough water in the system to float the stream. In spots there will be long, deep pools, and in other areas shallow gravel bars and rock gardens. You may need to drag your canoe over some of these shallow areas, or pick your way around exposed rocks, but it is quite a beautiful paddle. To find out if the generators are running, call the TVA Information Line at 1-800/238-2264. When the recording comes on, press (4) to access the water release schedule, then press (42) for Wilbur Dam. To find out the release schedule for the following day, press the (#) button. Remember, this is NOT a river to be run in an open canoe when the generators are running. A good section to paddle is between the iron bridge on Wilbur Dam Road in Siam to the next access bridge at Hwy 400 in Elizabethton. This is approximately five river miles. The folks who run the local rafting trips on the Watauga will allow canoers to put in at their access area with prior permission. This is a very nice facility just a mile or so upriver from the Siam bridge.

Directions: From Elizabethton, travel east on US 321 to Watauga Lake and boat launch areas. To access Watauga Dam and Watauga River, travel east on US 321 from Elizabethton for .6 miles to right turn on Siam Road. Bear left at 3.5 miles to stay on Siam; continue .6 miles and turn right on Wilbur Dam Road. Stay on this road until you reach the end at Watauga Dam.

Safety Considerations: AVOID WINDY CONDITIONS ON OPEN LAKE. POWERBOAT TRAFFIC MAY BE HEAVY DURING SUMMER SEASON.
Ownership: Tennessee Valley Authority
Resource Numbers:
United States Forest Service —423/735-1500
TVA Information Line — 1-800/238-2264
B-Cliff Whitewater Rafting — 423/542-2262

The remote Watauga Lake is surrounded by towering mountain peaks and lush forests.

The Appalachian Trail crosses Watauga Dam and then proceeds up the mountain ridge for a spectacular view of the lake below.

Several small islands on Watauga Lake are just right for camping or picnicking. Some of the land around the lake is privately owned — be sure to get permission before accessing these areas.

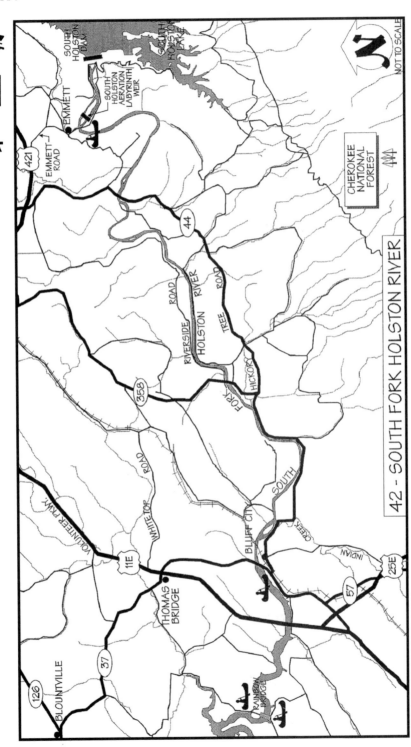

42 - SOUTH FORK HOLSTON RIVER

42 South Fork Holston River

USGS Quadrangles: Holston Valley, Bristol, Keenburg
Tennessee Atlas: Map 70, 71, 63

Size: 13 river miles from Bristol Waterworks Weir to Bluff City
Closest Town: Bristol   **County:** Sullivan
Best Time of Year: Year-round when generators are releasing

Description: Unfortunately for the Holston River, it has gained a repu-tation for being one of the most polluted industrial rivers in Tennessee. This is true, except for a small section that runs below the South Holston Dam, known as the South Holston Tailwater. This little stretch of Class I river is bright and clear, with small rapids and shoals, making it a pleasure to float at any time of year when the generators are releasing water. It is a fairly wide stretch of river, averaging 65 feet, with an occasional deadfall the only danger to navigation. The banks are steep and the scenery is pleasant. Dogwoods and wildflowers are very showy in the spring, and fall colors are brilliant in autumn. Several small islands are encountered along the 13 mile route that are just right for picnicking. An intermediate access point exists at the Weaver Pike Bridge in Riverside.

The South Fork Holston is a good area for spotting several exciting bird species. Common loons and grebe swim on Holston Lake above the dam, and bald eagles are beginning to make a comeback in the area. Plenty of fishing activity takes place on the South Fork Holston, but most-ly from the banks as fishermen angle for trout, white bass and striped bass.

To find out if the generators are running, and how many are running, call the TVA Information Line at 1-800/238-2264. When the recording comes on, press (4) to access the water release schedule, then press (01) for South Holston Dam. To find out the release schedule for the following day, press the (#) button. Make sure there is at least one generator run-ning before planning your trip. Water levels will rise quickly around the dam when water is first released. Use caution in this area.

Directions: From Bristol, take US 421 south to Emmett Road. Turn right onto Emmett and travel a short distance to left turn towards South Holston Aeration Labyrinth Weir. Put-in at canoe launch just over bridge.

Safety Considerations: STRAINERS AND DEADFALLS. WATER LEVELS RISE QUICKLY BELOW DAM AFTER RELEASE.
Ownership: Tennessee Valley Authority
Resource Numbers:
      TVA Information Line — 1-800/238-2264

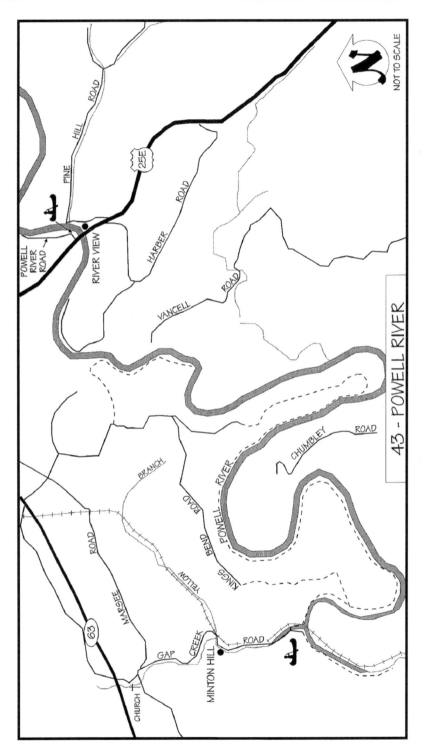

43 - POWELL RIVER

43 Powell River

USGS Quadrangles: Middlesburo South, Clouds
Tennessee Atlas: Map 68

Size: 10.6 miles from River View to Minton Hill
Closest Town: River View   **County:** Claiborne
Best Time of Year: Year-round except during dry periods

Description: The Powell River is one of those great finds — a river that has clean, clear water, superb fishing, excellent wildlife viewing, beautiful views, and no one on it! A good section to explore is a rather long stretch from the little community of River View, near the Kentucky-Tennessee-Virginia border, to the next access point at Minton Hill. On the other side of the river from the put-in, is a small monument that commemorates the Powell River Ferry that once operated at that location. It was built before the Civil War and used as a public toll crossing until 1905 when a wooden-floored bridge was erected.

This area of Tennessee is rugged and undeveloped. The terrain is mostly steep wooded banks with the Cumberland Mountains looming in the distance. One can continue to run the Powell River downstream into the Norris Lake reservoir, but there are long, remote stretches without any access just before reaching the lake. Burrowing mussels and worms thrive in the soft, muddy bottom, and turtles are abundant on every log. The Powell River has one of the largest populations of fresh-water mussels, including the endangered birdwing pearlymussel.

Directions: From La Follette, take Hwy 63 east to US 25 E. Turn right on US 25 E and drive 2.2 miles to left turn on Powell River Road. Put in at bottom of hill where road turns left and access road continues to river. To shuttle cars to take-out, take US 25 E back to Hwy 63. Turn left towards La Follette and drive 3.3 miles to small crossroad. Turn left on Gap Creek Road and stay on it as it parallels the scenic Gap Creek. (There is a confusing intersection just after turning onto Gap Creek Road in Minton Hill - be sure to take the middle fork just past the church and follow alongside Gap Creek.) Travel for 2.1 miles on one-lane road to the take-out by the Powell River. You can only park a few cars at this location.

Safety Considerations: STRAINERS AND DEADFALLS.
Ownership: Private
Resource Numbers: N/A

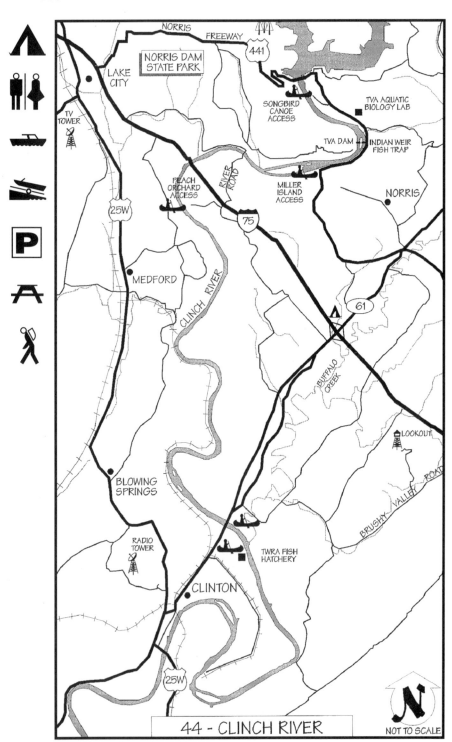

NORRIS DAM STATE PARK

NORRIS FREEWAY

441

LAKE CITY

TV TOWER

25W

PEACH ORCHARD ACCESS

RIVER ROAD

SONGBIRD CANOE ACCESS

TVA AQUATIC BIOLOGY LAB

TVA DAM

INDIAN WEIR FISH TRAP

MILLER ISLAND ACCESS

NORRIS

75

MEDFORD

CLINCH RIVER

61

BUFFALO CREEK

LOOKOUT

BLOWING SPRINGS

BRUSHY VALLEY ROAD

RADIO TOWER

TWRA FISH HATCHERY

CLINTON

25W

44 - CLINCH RIVER

NOT TO SCALE

Clinch River

USGS Quadrangles: Norris, Lake City
Tennessee Atlas: Map 59

Size: 10 miles from Miller Island Access to Hwy 61 Bridge
Closest Town: Norris   **County:** Anderson
Best Time of Year: Year-round when water is being released

Description: The Clinch River is a wide, meandering stream with cold, clean water flowing from the Norris Dam. With several good access areas and nice facilities, the Clinch is a highly recommended float stream. Although there is always a lot of activity on the banks as fishermen angle for brown and rainbow trout, the river itself is underused by canoers. Tall hillsides and occasional farmland make the scenery very pleasant with spring wildflowers visible along the banks and waterfowl in abundance on the river. Great blue herons, green-backed herons and gulls are frequently seen along the river. The River Bluff Hiking Trail that begins at the overlook above Norris Dam is a 3.2 mile loop, featuring Celandine poppies, Dutchman's breeches and trout lily in the spring. Another small hiking trail along the river is located at the Songbird Canoe Access just below the dam. Here you can expect to see northern and orchard orioles, eastern bluebirds and tree swallows.

An interesting stop is the TVA Aquatic Biology Headquarters located just before the Norris Dam on Norris Freeway. The lab has a fascinating display of freshwater mussels (you won't believe how many there are) and a complete collection of mounted fish. Biologists at the lab are very helpful in answering questions about local aquatic life, including horror stories about the exotic zebra mussels that are invading Tennessee waters.

Another nearby attraction is the Lenoir Museum and Grist Mill which is just down the road from the TVA Aquatic Biology Lab. Here you can see an old grist mill and raising barn. If this is of interest to you, then the nearby Museum of Appalachia is a another stop to add to your list. The living mountain village has displays, demonstrations, and pioneer crafts. It is located in the small community of Norris.

Since the floatability of the Clinch depends largely on the needs of TVA's hydroelectric system, you must be sure to call ahead before planning your trip. Although there is always some water in the river to insure that the aquatic life is not left high and dry, the river has little movement when no generators are running. Most paddlers prefer to canoe when at least one generator is discharging.

To find out if the generators are running, call the TVA Information Line at 1-800/238-2264. When the recording comes on, press (4) to access the water release schedule, then press (17) for the Norris Dam. To find out the release schedule for the following day, press the (#) button. Water levels will rise quickly around the dam when water is first released. Use caution in this area. If you use the Songbird Canoe Access area, you must portage your canoes around the TVA weir dam that is located less than a mile downstream.

When water is not releasing from the dam, a great alternate trip is to paddle any number of small coves and creeks that feed into Norris Lake. Cove Creek, Cedar Creek and Big Creek are just a few. The nearby Big Ridge State Park has boat ramps into Norris lake as well as camping facilities. Norris Lake, like the Clinch River, is one of the clearest water systems in the state. This is one of the few lakes that is popular with scuba divers in the summer months.

Directions: From I-75 north of Knoxville, take exit 122 (Norris/Clinton). Turn right (east) on Hwy 61 for 1.4 miles to left turn on US 441 (Norris Fwy.) Take this all the way to Norris Dam or turn left at River Road to Miller Island Access. To shuttle cars to the take-out, travel back to Hwy 61, turn right and drive to take-out under bridge. A shorter trip can be made by putting in at Peach Orchard Access.

Safety Considerations: AVOID WINDY CONDITIONS ON LAKE. DEADFALLS AND STRAINERS MAY BE PRESENT. WATER LEVELS RISE QUICKLY WHEN GENERATORS ARE TURNED ON. WATER BELOW DAM IS EXTREMELY COLD.

Ownership: Tennessee Valley Authority

Resource Numbers:
TVA Information Line —
1-800/238-2264
Museum of Appalachia —
865/494-7680
Big Ridge State Park —
865/992-5523 or
1-800/471-5305

Paddling the open waters of Norris Lake is a nice option when generators are not supplying water for the Clinch River below Norris Dam.

In the spring, wildflowers abound along the Clinch River. Rare Virginia bluebells are found in the early spring.

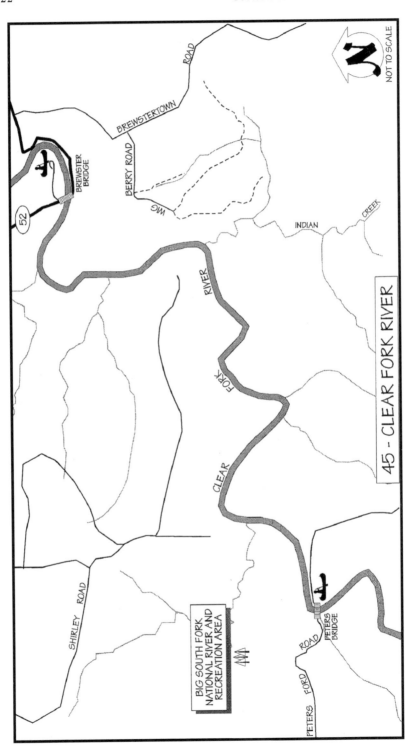

NOT TO SCALE

BREWSTERTOWN ROAD

BERRY ROAD

BREWSTER BRIDGE

52

WIG

INDIAN CREEK

RIVER

FORK

CLEAR

45 - CLEAR FORK RIVER

SHIRLEY ROAD

BIG SOUTH FORK NATIONAL RIVER AND RECREATION AREA

PETERS ROAD

PETERS BRIDGE

PETERS FORD

45 Clear Fork River

USGS Quadrangles: Rugby, Burrville
Tennessee Atlas: Map 57, 58

Size: 6 river miles from Peters Ford Bridge to Brewster Bridge
Closest Town: Rugby   **County:** Fentress, Morgan
Best Time of Year: Year-round

Description: Make no mistake about it, the Clear Fork River is not a beginner's stream. It is, however, the only river of the 125,000 acre Big South Fork National River and Recreation Area that is qualified to be included in this guide due to its generally tame nature and, of course, its undeniable beauty. The Big South Fork area of the Cumberland Plateau is chock-full of spectacular rivers. Unfortunately, for the novice they are almost all fast and technical — some are downright insane. But if you are looking to get your feet wet (and maybe your whole body) on a Class II river — this should be the one.

Clear Fork is free-flowing, clean and exceptionally scenic. It is remote and thickly-vegetated with rhododendron, mountain laurel and hemlock. Lots of shoals, small waterfalls cascading down rock walls and riverside bluffs complete the picture — it's gorgeous. Small caves under the riverside cliffs, called rockhouses, were once used by Indians as shelters. Beyond the take-out at Brewster Bridge, on the next section of Clear Fork, and just before the confluence of White Oak Creek, is an area known locally as The Gentlemen's Swimming Hole. This rock-bottom pool was once used by the residents of Rugby back in the 1800's when their self-sufficient little settlement was in its heyday. A hiking trail off of Hwy 52 leads to this historic recreation area.

A noteworthy aspect of Clear Fork River is that the more water it has in it, the less difficult it becomes. As more water flows over the rocks, the technical rapids wash out. It is also runnable Year-round while other rivers of the Cumberland Plateau depend on seasonal rain. Look for the sleek river otter or predatory mink that are sometimes seen on the river. An enormous quantity of fish species, including colorful darters can be seen, as well as rare and endangered mussels. Because of its remoteness, this is also a good place to view coyote, wild boar and — hopefully — the black bear, which may soon be reintroduced here.

Directions: From I-40 north of Crossville, take US 127 north for 30 miles to Hwy 296. Turn right on Hwy 296 and go 2.5 miles to stop sign. Continue east on Hwy 52 for 3 miles to right turn on Peters Ford Road. Put-in at Peters Ford Bridge over Clear Fork River. To shuttle cars to take-out, travel back to Hwy 52, turn right and continue for 6.5 miles to

Brewster Bridge.

Safety Considerations: STRAINERS AND DEADFALLS. FLASH-
FLOODING.
Ownership: Big South Fork National River and Recreation Area (BSFN-
RA)
Resource Numbers:
    BSFNRA — 423/286-7275

The poisonous cottonmouth water moccasin was so named because of the white flesh inside its mouth, which it reveals when threatened. Because these snakes become aggressive when agitated, they should be left alone.

Finding a lunch spot on Clear Fork River is easy with many big boulders to choose from.